NEW NELSON HISTORY

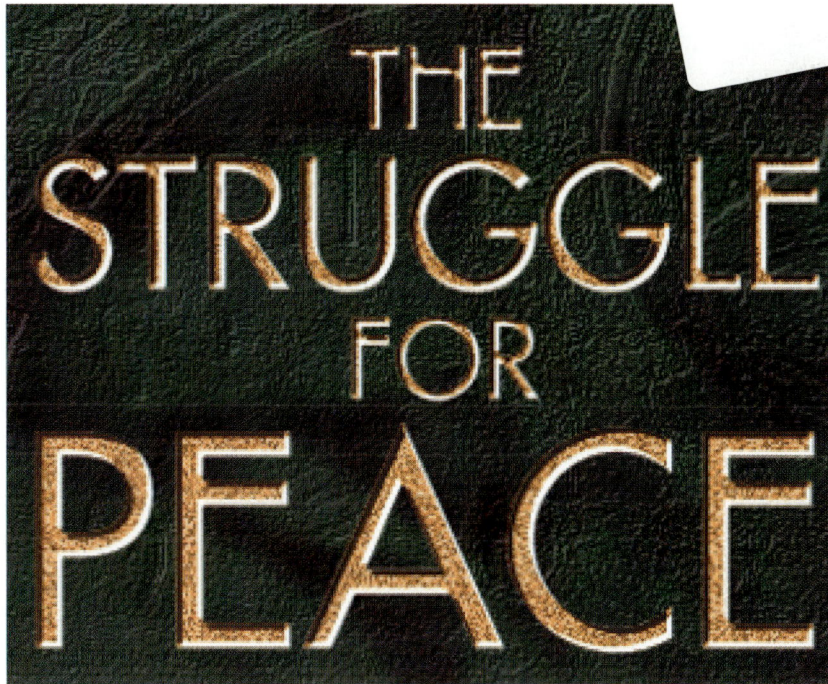

THE STRUGGLE FOR PEACE

1918-1989

JOHN TRAYNOR AND IAN DAWSON

Nelson

Acquisitions: Roda Morrison
Administration: Eileen Regan
Editorial: Clare Haworth-Maden
Marketing: Jeremy Warner
Picture research: Image Select International Ltd
Production: Ros Moon
Project management: Jessica Hodge
Staff design: Lorraine Inglis
Typesetting: Sharon Rudd

Thomas Nelson and Sons Ltd
Nelson House Mayfield Road
Walton-on-Thames Surrey
KT12 5PL UK

Thomas Nelson Australia
102 Dodds Street
South Melbourne
Victoria 3205 Australia

Nelson Canada
1120 Birchmount Road
Scarborough Ontario
M1K 5G4 Canada

© Ian Dawson and John Traynor 1997

First published by Thomas Nelson and Sons Ltd 1997

I⊕P®   Thomas Nelson is an
        International Thomson Publishing Company

I⊕P®   is used under licence

ISBN 0-17-4351062
NPN 9 8 7 6 5 4 3 2 1

Acknowledgements
The publishers are grateful to the following for permission to reproduce copyright material:

AKG: 46, 50, 51 right, 58, 68 left, 72, 82, 86, 90, 93 bottom, 111 bottom
Corbis: 87
Hulton Getty Picture Collection Ltd: 17 right, 42 left and right, 47, 52, 61, 62, 69, 70, 71 left, 79 left and
right, 91, 94 top, 105, 106, 108/9, 110, 112 top and bottom, 116 top, 118
Image Select International Ltd: 11, 12, 51 left, 56, 71 bottom right, 74, 83 (Xinhua Chine Nouv), 102
(Halstead), 107, 120 bottom left (Mingam) and bottom right (Daniel Simon), 122 (Christian Vioujard),
124 (Vladimir Chech)
John Frost Newspapers: 114
Mary Evans Picture Library: 6, 13, 71 top right, 85, 88/9
Novosti: 68 right, 126
Popperfoto: 4, 5, 17 left, 54, 73, 78, 81, 84, 92, 93 top, 95, 96/7, 98 left and right, 99, 111 top, 113,
115, 116 bottom, 120 top, 125
Rex: 127
Spectrum: 9

Text extracts: Guardian Newspapers Ltd, 6; Simon and Schuster Inc., 99

Every effort has been made to trace all copyright holders, but if any have been inadvertently
overlooked, the publishers will be pleased to make the necessary arrangements at the first opportunity.

Printed in Croatia

Contents

1 The conflicts of a lifetime

On 2 June 1913, George Dawson was born. Two days later, a young woman called Emily Davison was standing among thousands of spectators watching the racehorses in the Derby. Suddenly she leapt out, flinging herself under the hooves of the king's horse. Emily died. Her death was her protest against the politicians who refused to let women vote in general elections.

Young George was born into a troubled country. Suffragettes were demanding the vote. Ireland was on the brink of civil war. Striking workers demanded fair wages and better working conditions. Poverty and ill-health were rife. Over 100 in every 1000 babies died before their first birthday, and the average life expectancy was only a little over fifty years.

Worse was to come: in August 1914 World War I began. George's father joined the army and scarcely saw his son again until George was past his fifth birthday. His father was lucky, however, surviving the horrors of trench warfare to return home. In 1918 politicians promised the returning soldiers 'Homes fit for Heroes', and promised women the vote. At least the women got what they were promised.

During the 1920s and 1930s, George's father struggled to find a regular job. Unemployment was common. George was clever. He won a scholarship to the Liverpool Institute, but there was no money to go to university. When he left school he worked as a clerk, but spent more time thinking about cricket and football.

Even a sports-mad young man, however, could not help noticing that another war was looming closer.

Adolf Hitler had seized power in Germany in 1933 and was rebuilding the German army. One by one, the countries bordering Germany were taken over. In September 1939 Hitler's troops invaded Poland. Britain and France declared war on Germany.

George joined the army immediately. He spent the early war years in Britain, like everyone else, waiting for the expected German invasion. It never came but, in 1941, Japan joined the war. George found himself in India and then in Burma. During the years after the war he scarcely told his family anything about that time, of sweating through jungles and swamps, rifle and bayonet at the ready, not knowing where the enemy was, or when it would attack.

Some of the fiercest fighting of World War II took place in Burma. Many of the soldiers felt that they were the 'Forgotten Army', however, because far more publicity was given to the war in Europe.

Timeline – main events of twentieth century covered in book

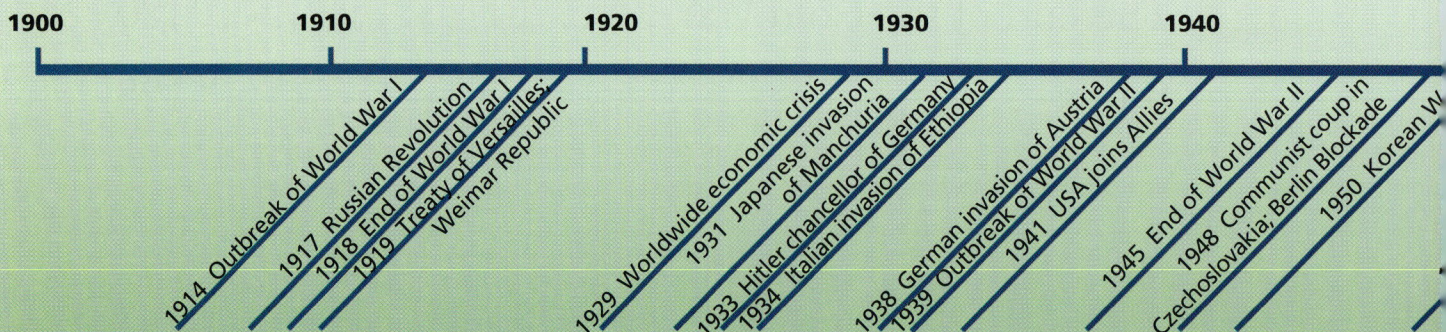

1900	1910	1920	1930	1940

1914 Outbreak of World War I
1917 Russian Revolution
1918 End of World War I
1919 Treaty of Versailles; Weimar Republic
1929 Worldwide economic crisis
1931 Japanese invasion of Manchuria
1933 Hitler chancellor of Germany
1934 Italian invasion of Ethiopia
1938 German invasion of Austria
1939 Outbreak of World War II
1941 USA joins Allies
1945 End of World War II
1948 Communist coup in Czechoslovakia; Berlin Blockade
1950 Korean War

George's war ended in 1945, when the atomic bombs were dropped on Hiroshima and Nagasaki. Yet, as millions like George settled into peacetime, the USA and the USSR were growing ever more hostile. As their fear of each other grew, each built up an arsenal of nuclear weapons. In 1962 it seemed that World War III was imminent.

President Kennedy of the USA demanded that the USSR remove its missiles from the island of Cuba, off the American coast. Khrushchev, the Soviet leader, refused. Anxious families all over the world listened to news bulletins, fearing that their children would not live to be adults. Even children, who were supposed to know nothing about politics, felt the tension. Then Khrushchev backed down, and the missiles were taken away. The world breathed again.

That was not the end of the Cold War, however: the USSR and the USA took sides in many small conflicts, and raced each other to build bigger bombs, and to reach the moon. While conflict simmered, George's family lived more and more comfortably. George bought luxuries that his parents could not have afforded, even if they had been invented: a fridge, washing machine and television in the 1950s, a car in the 1960s. His family took holidays in faraway places – like Devon. The National Health Service gave people free medicine and treatment. By the 1980s, fewer than 20 babies in every 1000 died before the age of one. Life expectancy increased to over seventy years.

The conflicts that had loomed over George's life seemed to have ended in 1989. President Gorbachev of the USSR wanted peace. The Berlin Wall was torn down. Fear of war ebbed away but did not disappear completely, however. A host of smaller conflicts broke out, ensuring there was no peaceful ending to the conflicts of a lifetime.

The greatest symbol of the Cold War was the Berlin Wall, which was built in 1961 to stop East Germans from fleeing to the West.

QUESTIONS

1 **Which countries fought both of the world wars?**

2 **Who was on each side during the Cold War?**

3 **When did people have the greatest fear of a third world war?**

4 **Write down as many reasons as you can think of why the twentieth century has been so full of conflicts. (It may help to think about the reasons for current conflicts.)**

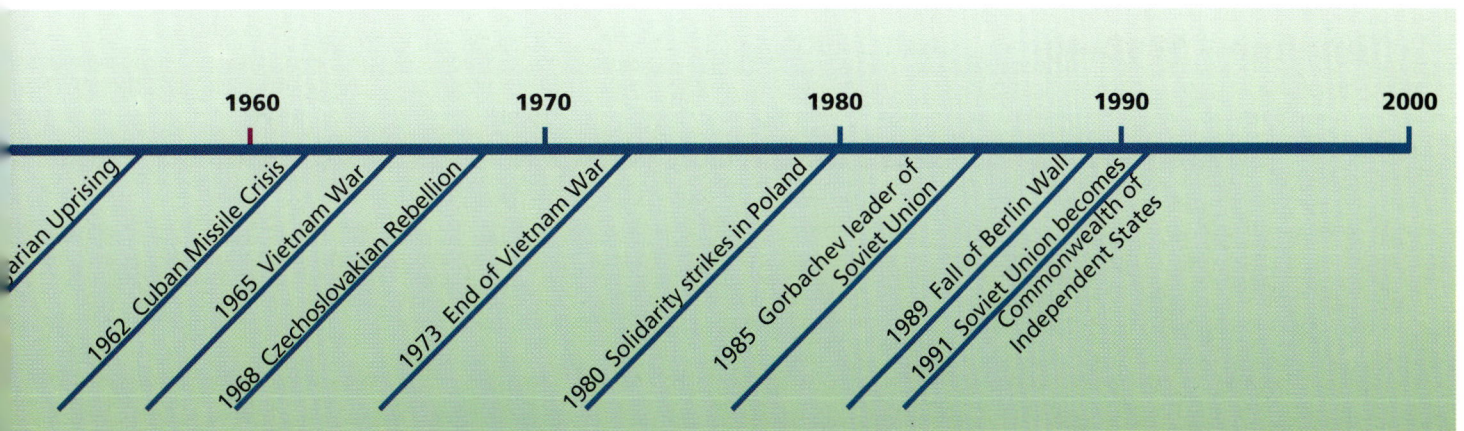

1960   1970   1980   1990   2000

...arian Uprising

1962 Cuban Missile Crisis

1965 Vietnam War

1968 Czechoslovakian Rebellion

1973 End of Vietnam War

1980 Solidarity strikes in Poland

1985 Gorbachev leader of Soviet Union

1989 Fall of Berlin Wall

1991 Soviet Union becomes Commonwealth of Independent States

Why did World War II begin?

At five o'clock this morning a sharp and heavy bombardment crashed down on the enemy lines in France. It lasted a mere fifteen minutes. Then over went the tanks. In great force they went through a dense fog that persisted for two hours and more after dawn. But for the fog I think the attack might have failed.

Behind them on our front went the Canadians with fixed bayonets. Later, when the sun shone through, we who were following saw the consequences – the horses dead in shafts, held up only by their halters still tied to posts where they were delivering rations; half-clothed men stuck like pigs while running away; mixed groups of young and old soldiers huddled in death beside their guns and one pathetic brotherhood of corpses in a sunken road with bayonet wounds already black with flies.

The defeat became a rout. Batteries of guns with dumps of shells were abandoned. Even our supply tanks, mine among them, were soon miles behind enemy lines … Their machine gunners, many of them mere boys and chained to their guns, died in ditches where we splashed them with mud as we passed. On we went … through old battlefields until at last the eleventh hour struck on the eleventh day of the eleventh month and it was over.

Not too soon. Even in that last hour men died. I saw one lying by the roadside; he looked very young and lonely.

An account of the end of World War I by an English soldier, B A Steward, printed in *The Guardian* in 1991.

I t may seem strange to begin work on the causes of World War II by reading about the end of World War I. This isn't a mistake: the two wars were connected. World War I lasted so long that it was known as the 'The Great War'. In 1918, more optimistically, people called it 'the war to end all wars' – but they were wrong. Twenty years later, another war began in Europe, which spread even more widely and lasted even longer. The first half of this book investigates why World War II began. Was it linked to World War I, or did new reasons arise for its cause during the 1920s and 1930s?

A romanticised artist's view of the poppy fields of Flanders where so many men lost their lives.

Timeline – 1918–40

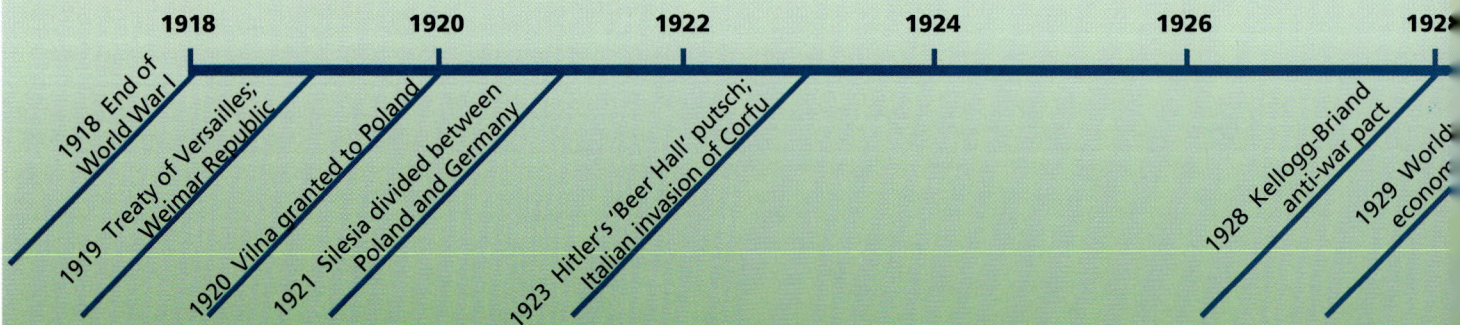

1918 · 1920 · 1922 · 1924 · 1926 · 192[8]

- 1918 End of World War I
- 1919 Treaty of Versailles; Weimar Republic
- 1920 Vilna granted to Poland
- 1921 Silesia divided between Poland and Germany
- 1923 Hitler's 'Beer Hall' putsch; Italian invasion of Corfu
- 1928 Kellogg-Briand anti-war pact
- 1929 World[econom[

Why did World War II begin?

World War II was caused by the peace treaty that ended World War I. Many Germans felt that the Treaty of Versailles was very unfair, stripping Germany of land, people and wealth. After that there was bound to be another war because Germany wanted to restore the balance.

World War II could have been prevented if the League of Nations had worked properly. The league was set up to prevent wars, but powerful countries such as the USA and the USSR did not join the league. If the league had been more powerful, it could have stopped German aggression in the 1930s.

World War II began because the German leader, Adolf Hitler, wanted to conquer Europe and create a German empire. Hitler wanted glory for himself and Germany and would not be stopped by anyone.

Historian A   **Historian B**   **Historian C**

QUESTIONS

1 **Explain in your own words the three ideas about why World War II began.**

2 **Can you suggest connections between the causes put forward by:**

   a historians A and C;
   b historians B and C?

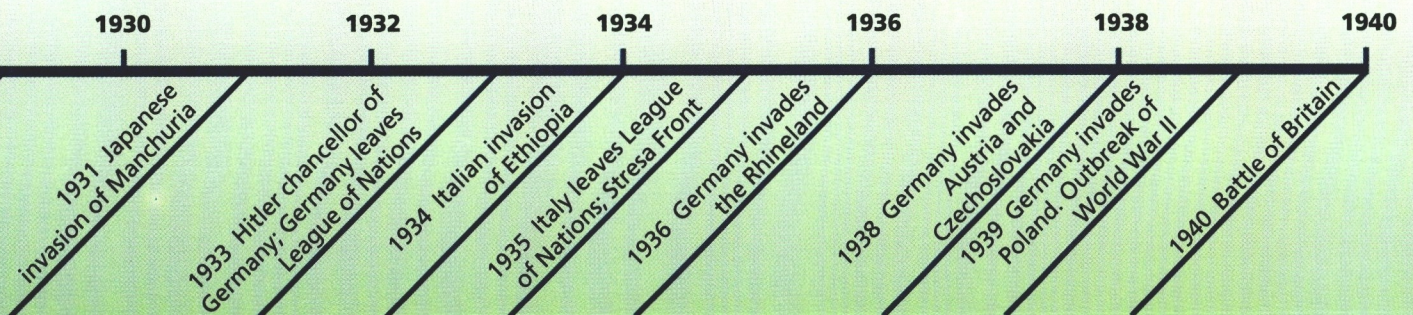

1930   1932   1934   1936   1938   1940

1931 Japanese invasion of Manchuria

1933 Hitler chancellor of Germany; Germany leaves League of Nations

1934 Italian invasion of Ethiopia

1935 Italy leaves League of Nations; Stresa Front

1936 Germany invades the Rhineland

1938 Germany invades Austria and Czechoslovakia

1939 Germany invades Poland. Outbreak of World War II

1940 Battle of Britain

3 The Great War, 1914–18

On 28 June 1914, in the town of Sarajevo in Bosnia, a young man called Gavrilo Princip loaded his revolver and took aim. His target was the heir to the Austro-Hungarian empire, Archduke Franz Ferdinand. Princip fired. The archduke and his wife fell, mortally wounded.

News of the assassination appeared in newspapers all over Europe. In Britain, many holiday-makers glanced at the story as they sat on the beach or watched cricket. The distant shooting did not seem to affect them but, within weeks, Princip's bullets would set the countries of Europe tumbling into war, like a row of falling dominoes.

In 1914, as a result of many rivalries and jealousies, Europe was split into two armed groups. Britain, France and Russia faced Germany and Austria-Hungary. Britain had the largest and oldest empire, but Germany was rapidly increasing her power, and building up her navy. Each country wondered whether the other was about to attack it.

Caught between the two armed groups was Serbia. Austria-Hungary threatened Serbia because Princip, the assassin of Austria-Hungary's archduke, was a Serb. Russia stepped in to protect Serbia and declared war on Austria-Hungary. Austria-Hungary's ally, Germany, retaliated by declaring war on Russia and her ally, France. This was a dangerous move for Germany, because it did not want to fight both countries at the same time.

Germany therefore planned to defeat France quickly, by sending its army around the edge of the French defences through Belgium, and then attacking the encircled country. It was the German invasion of Belgium that brought Britain into the war because Britain had made a treaty in 1839 promising to prevent anyone invading Belgium, and Britain thus declared war on Germany on 4 August 1914.

Crowds outside Buckingham Palace cheered the news of war: nearly everyone thought that Britain had to fight the Kaiser's army in order to stop Germany from taking over Europe. At the same time, people expected the war to be over by Christmas. Young men rushed to be part of this great adventure, to have their 'crack at the Hun'.

The alliances of 1914

Central powers

Entente powers

0   500   1000 km
0   250   500 miles

NORTH SEA
BRITAIN
NORTH ATLANTIC
HOLLAND
BELGIUM
GERMANY
RUSSIA
FRANCE
SWITZERLAND
AUSTRIA-HUNGARY
ITALY
PORTUGAL
SPAIN
SERBIA
TURKEY
MEDITERRANEAN SEA
N

After the war, even the smallest villages put up memorials to their men who had been killed in the war. Today it can be astonishing to visit some little villages and to see twenty, thirty or more names of those who never came back listed on the memorials. In many places, large groups of friends joined the army together (in towns, 'Pals' battalions were recruited): they died together too. After a 'big push', every house in a street might receive a telegram giving news of a wounded or dead son or husband.

Many men also wanted to escape from their humdrum jobs. Lance Corporal H Fellows said that he joined up because 'I was very poor and had never had a holiday in my life. I chose to join the Northumberland Fusiliers because it gave me the longest train ride'. Many recruits were under-age. Corporal J Norton explained why: 'I was a member of the village cricket and football teams and nearly everyone of their members enlisted. I was only 16, but I tried to join up too. The recruiting sergeant asked me my age and, when I told him, he said "you had better go out, come in again and tell me different". I came back, told him I was 19, and I was in'.

Trench warfare

The war was not over by Christmas, although Germany almost won in the first months when the fighting was happening fast. The small British Expeditionary Force was pushed aside, and the French army managed to stop the Germans only miles from Paris. In December 1914 the two opposing armies faced each other, each determined not to give ground. They began to dig defensive trenches for mile after mile through the countryside of northern France and Belgium. Trench warfare was a new kind of war. Earlier wars had seen cavalry charges against cannon, and men advancing against rifles and bayonets. In this war, however, the key weapon was the machine gun: from their trenches, which were protected by barbed wire, machine gunners could mow down enemy soldiers as they advanced across 'no-man's land'. Horses, which had been a vital part of warfare for hundreds of years, were suddenly obsolete, of no use.

Perhaps the worst day of all was 1 July 1916, the first day of the Battle of the Somme. For days the British gunners had been firing at the German trenches, confident that their shells would destroy the Germans' wire and machine guns and thus force their troops to retreat; in theory, British troops would simply have to walk across no-man's land to victory. That day 60,000 British soldiers were killed or wounded. These are the words of some of the survivors, recorded in Martin Middlebrook's book, *The First Day on the Somme*.

As we advanced out of our trenches the sun was shining gloriously and it seemed that every bird in the sky was trying to out-sing the noise of the guns.

As the gunfire died away I saw an infantryman climb onto the parapet into no-man's land, beckoning others to follow. As he did so he kicked off a football; a good kick, the ball rose and travelled well towards the German line. That seemed to be the signal to advance. For some reason nothing seemed to happen to us at first;

we strolled along as though walking in a park. Then, suddenly, we were in the midst of a storm of machine-gun bullets and I saw men beginning to twirl round and fall in all kinds of curious ways as they were hit – quite unlike the way actors do in films.

It was about this time that my feeling of confidence was replaced by an acceptance of the fact that I had been sent here to die.

Attitudes to the war

Despite such failures, support for the war continued. One soldier wrote home that he wanted to destroy 'this race of evil human devils'. Yet many soldiers realised that the men that they were fighting were really just like them: ordinary men with parents, wives and children. They had to fight because 'orders were orders', but they did not hate the soldiers on the other side. One English soldier wrote to his family:

The German that I shot who died soon afterwards was a fine-looking man. I was there when he died, poor chap. I did feel sorry, but it was my life or his; he was speaking but none of us could understand a word he said, to tell you the truth I had a tear myself, I thought to myself, perhaps he has a mother or dad, also a sweetheart, and a lot of things like that, I was really sorry I did it, but God knows I could not help myself.

Most people at home did not understand such attitudes. Because they had not seen the suffering in both sets of trenches, they found it easy to believe that all Germans were evil. People at home felt bitter because of the high casualties and the disruption to their daily lives that the war was causing. For the first time in history the whole population was involved in war. Thousands of workers, including many women, were making weapons and ammunition.

The end of the war

Month after month, year after year, the war continued. There had been longer wars before, but never one with such long, continuous fighting. New weapons such as tanks, aeroplanes and gas were used, but they could not break through the lines of machine guns. In 1917 the USA entered the war, providing fresh men and equipment. This help was greatly needed, for in the same year Russia made peace with Germany, after the Communist revolution had overthrown the tsar.

Germany made a final effort early in 1918. After years of fighting for just yards of land, the German army broke through the Allied lines, but was then too exhausted to force a victory. In Germany itself, food supplies were very short, and people were desperate for peace. Allied troops won back the lost ground and launched their own attack in August. In November 1918 the German army surrendered, the Kaiser abdicated, and the war ended. The only silver lining seemed to be that such a horrific war must have been 'the war to end all wars'. In 1919 the victorious countries met in Paris, at the Palace of Versailles, to agree the peace treaty. The future peace of the world seemed to depend on their decision.

◄ D A T A P O I N T ►

The impact of World War 1

1 Total number of deaths

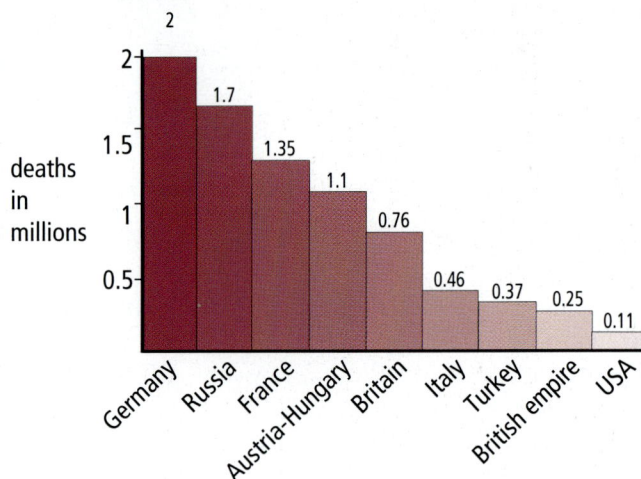

2 Proportion of forces killed or wounded

	% dead	% wounded	% unhurt
Britain	12	27	59
France	14	53	29

3 Deaths per day compared with other wars

World War I (1914–18)	5,509
Boer War (1899–1902)	10
American Civil War (1861–65)	518
Crimean War (1853–56)	1,075
Napoleonic Wars (1793–1815)	233

The leaders of the three major countries which decided on the content of the Treaty of Versailles: from right, Woodrow Wilson of the USA, Georges Clemenceau of France and David Lloyd George of Britain, with Vittorio Orlando of Italy on the left.

QUESTIONS

1 Which event was the immediate cause of the war?

2 Why were Britain and Germany suspicious of each other?

3 Why did Britain declare war in 1914?

4 Why was it difficult for the armies to make breakthroughs?

5 Which new weapons were used during the war?

6 Which countries suffered the most casualties?

7 How did World War I compare with earlier wars?

How did people react to the Great War?

SOURCE A

A soldier lies dead in a trench after the Battle of Champagne in 1915.

SOURCE C

I want to go home, I want to go home,

I don't want to go to the trenches no more

Where whizzbangs and shrapnel they whistle and roar,

Take me over the sea where the alleyman can't get at me.

Oh my, I don't want to die, I want to go home.

A soldiers' song (alleyman was slang for German).

SOURCE B

… on the next morning, after being made to drink a lot of rum, I went over the top for the first time. Everybody has written about it and nobody can describe it. Not really. The legs and the arms of the dead stretched out, the ripped bellies of the horses steaming and stinking. And the dead faces of mates looking up at you out of the filth. Filth. Men made into filth before your very eyes.

The memories of a soldier, quoted in Ronald Blythe's, *The View in Winter* (1979). The soldier told his story when he was 79.

SOURCE D

I hope to God the politicians in England will not betray us and make peace before we have absolutely crushed our enemies, and made a repetition of this hellish business impossible. To make peace before this is done would be a criminal betrayal of the Living and the Dead. Modern war is hell, and we must make a recurrence of it impossible for all generations, come what may.

An entry in 1916 from the diary of Lieutenant William St Leger, a British officer killed in 1918, aged 23.

SOURCE E

A drawing of the two-minute silence at 11.00a.m. on 11 November 1919. For many years after 1918 people commemorated the ending of the Great War at the precise moment that it had ended (not on the nearest Sunday, as happened later). Even in city centres, transport stopped and people stopped working. There was utter silence.

QUESTIONS

1 Do you think that Source A gives reliable evidence about trench warfare?

2 Is Source B more reliable than Source A about fighting conditions?

3 What can you learn from Sources A and B about fighting in the trenches?

4 Is Source C useful evidence about soldiers' attitudes to the war?

5 Read Source D. Was St Leger's attitude to the war the same as that of the soldiers who sang the song in Source C?

6 What does Source E tell you about people's attitudes to war?

7 Using as many sources as you wish, explain why people were determined that the Great War should be the 'war to end all wars'.

Did the Treaty of Versailles cause World War II?

Talks about the peace treaty to end World War I began in January 1919 at the Palace of Versailles, near Paris in France. The three leading figures present were President Woodrow Wilson of the USA, David Lloyd George, prime minister of Britain, and the French prime minister, Georges Clemenceau. Italy and Japan had also fought against Germany, but although they sent their leaders to Versailles, they were not as influential as the 'Big Three'. German leaders did not take part in the discussions; this was not a treaty negotiated between winners and losers. Instead, Germany had no choice but to accept the unconditional treaty that was decided by the winners.

When they began, the peace talks were surprisingly disorganised; there was no clear programme of discussions, and the leaders zigzagged from one topic to another. Everything depended on their respective enthusiasms and arguments. The three men did not get on well, however. When Wilson fell ill, Clemenceau delightedly told Lloyd George, 'he is worse today'. Later, the 78-year-old Clemenceau

> World War II was caused by the peace treaty that ended World War I. Many Germans felt that the Treaty of Versailles was very unfair, stripping Germany of land, people and wealth. After that there was bound to be another war because Germany wanted to restore the balance.

Historian A

This chapter will help you to work out whether this historian is right. The Treaty of Versailles of 1919 was certainly an important part of the background that led to the outbreak of World War II, but was it the most important cause?

The causes of World War II

SOURCE A

… the settlement that emerged from the months of deliberation at Paris was a creditable achievement. The fact that it did not survive the 1920s intact stemmed … not so much from the terms of the peace treaties themselves, but from the reluctance of political leaders of the interwar period to enforce them.

Ruth Henig, *Versailles and After, 1919-1933,* 1995.

SOURCE B

Germany fought specifically in the Second World War to reverse the verdict of the first and to destroy the settlement which followed it.

A J P Taylor, *The Origins of the Second World War,* 1961.

QUESTIONS

1 Which of the historians quoted in Sources A and B agrees with words of the historian at the top of the page?

2 What does the other historian believe about:
   a the terms of the Treaty of Versailles;
   b the reasons why the treaty was not kept?

threatened to attack Lloyd George after a disagreement. One of the most amusing scenes of the conference, described by an American delegate, took place in Mr Wilson's drawing-room in Paris, with the president on all fours on the floor in front of a large map, and Orlando (the Italian leader) crawling like a bear to get a better view.

There were also other reasons why the politicians faced a tremendously difficult task. The Great War had been the greatest horror that the world had ever known. Everyone wanted peace in the future, but many (particularly in France, which had suffered most and where the meeting was held) also wanted revenge on the country that they blamed for the war – Germany. Were both peace and revenge possible? The politicians also had to work quickly; the old Austro-Hungarian empire had already split up, and new countries were emerging. They needed to make sure that the new situation did not create more wars.

The treaty was signed on 28 June 1919 by the German leaders. Then the politicians moved on to deal with the treaties with the other countries that had fought alongside Germany. These treaties (see Datapoint, The treaties of 1919-20) were signed at other country houses (which gave the treaties their names) around Paris in 1919 and 1920.

◄ DATAPOINT ►

Extracts from the diary of Frances Stevenson, Lloyd George's secretary

10 March 1919
The Queen of Romania] spoke of meeting President Wilson on his arrival. 'What shall I talk to him about?' she asked. 'The League of Nations or my pink chemise?' 'Begin with the League of Nations', said Mr Balfour, 'and finish up with the pink chemise. If you were talking to Mr Lloyd George, you could begin with the pink chemise!'

14 March 1919
President Wilson arrived and D says he can think and talk of nothing else but his League of Nations. D says that everything must hang on that for him to take any interest in it ... [Wilson] has started to annoy D already by talking of matters that have already been settled as though they were still open for discussion and as though he intended to re-open them.

19 March 1919
'France is a poor winner', says D. 'She does not take her victories well.' The real reason, I think, is that the French are terrified at a repetition of 1914. They cannot believe that Germany is defeated, and feel that they cannot have enough guarantees for the future.

24 March 1919
D arrived back ... with all his plans made. He means business this week, and will sweep all before him. He will stand no more nonsense either from French or Americans. He is taking the long view about the Peace, and insists that it should be one that will not leave bitterness for years to come, and probably lead to another war.

5 April 1919
President Wilson in bed, but the meetings went on just the same. Clemenceau is very pleased at Wilson's absence, and could not conceal his joy. 'He is worse today', he said to D and doubled up with laughter. 'Do you know his doctor? Couldn't you get him round and bribe him?' The old man did not attempt to conceal his feelings on the subject.

28 June 1919
Went to Versailles for the signature of the Peace. Though I am glad I was there, yet the thing as a whole was very disappointing ... Almost half the room was taken up with representatives of the Press. The Press is reducing everything that is noblest and impressive in modern life into terms of Press photographs and Press interviews. In fact they try to dominate everything ... They are as unscrupulous as they are vulgar.

29 June 1919
D had a wonderful reception at the station [in London]. I think he had an idea that his reception would be rather a wash-out ... but the welcome he had was far more spontaneous than any organisation could have made it, and to crown all, the king himself, with the Prince of Wales, came to the station to meet him ... Everyone threw flowers at D.

The treaties of 1919-20

The Treaty of	with	date
Versailles	Germany	1919
St Germain	Austria	1919
Trianon	Hungary	1920
Sèvres	Turkey	1920
Neuilly	Bulgaria	1919

President Wilson's Fourteen Points

In January 1918 President Wilson had drawn up a list of fourteen points that he thought would make the basis for a fair treaty. At that stage Germany still expected to win the war, and rejected Wilson's ideas. At Versailles, however, Wilson still believed that his fourteen points could be the foundation of the peace treaty. Grouped together, his fourteen points covered three basic principles.

- Every nation or people had the right to govern themselves rather than being ruled by another country. This was known as the right to 'self-determination'. (Points 5–13)
- The chances of war would be reduced if countries cut their numbers of weapons and were open and fair with each other. (Points 1–4)
- A 'general association of nations', called the League of Nations, should be set up to settle disputes between countries peacefully. (Point 14)

Yet the politicians could not simply turn Wilson's Fourteen Points into a treaty. Indeed, by the time of Versailles, Wilson had himself changed his mind about his attitude to Germany; he had been angry when Germany had rejected his peace plan, and had been angrier still when Germany had then forced Russia to accept a harsh peace treaty (the Treaty of Brest-Litovsk) when Russia left the war. In 1919, Wilson was not feeling as lenient as in 1918.

◄ D A T A P O I N T ►

President Wilson's Fourteen Points

1. There should be no more secret treaties between countries. All governments should know what others had agreed.

2. No country should close waterways or stop another country's ships.

3. Countries should abolish customs duties on goods exported from one country to another.

4. All countries should cut their number of weapons.

5. The wishes of the people living in colonies should be considered when colonies were dealt with in the talks.

6. German forces must leave Russia.

7. Belgium must be independent.

8. Alsace-Lorraine must be returned to France.

9. Italy's borders should be altered to prevent disputes with Austria and to allow national groups within Italy to rule themselves.

10. There should be self-determination for the people of Eastern Europe, so allowing them to govern themselves.

11. The countries of Serbia, Romania and Montenegro should be restored.

12. There should be self-determination for the people of the Turkish empire, thus allowing them to govern themselves.

13. Poland should be independent of Russia.

14. A League of Nations should be set up to settle disputes between countries peacefully.

Clemenceau

Aged 78 at the time of the Treaty of Versailles, Clemenceau had bitter memories of the German victory in the 1870 Franco-Prussian (German) War, as a result of which Germany had taken the rich lands of Alsace-Lorraine from France.

The whole of France was bitter at the destruction of French farmland, industry and lives during World War I. Nearly 1.4 million French soldiers had died, and only 29 per cent of her troops had escaped death or wounding. The French Chamber of Deputies contained so many severely wounded ex-soldiers that it was known as the 'one-legged chamber'.

Clemenceau wanted – and the French people expected – the treaty to:
- punish Germany severely;
- take revenge for French losses through German compensation in money and land. This would help to repay the huge loans that France had taken out in order to pay for the war effort;
- protect France against future German attacks.

What were the peacemakers trying to achieve?

At the negotiations for the Treaty of Versailles, each of the 'Big Three' had its own objectives. They agreed on some issues but, inevitably, not on everything.

These pages show you what each leader – Clemenceau, Lloyd George and Wilson – was trying to achieve, and who they had to please.

Lloyd George

Lloyd George personally believed that the most important task of the peace conference was to prevent any future wars. Therefore he did not think that Germany should be punished too severely in case it later tried to overturn the treaty by force.

Lloyd George also believed that Britain needed Germany to recover from the war quickly and to become a prosperous country once more. This was vital for British trade, because Germany had been a major buyer of British exports. Now that the war was over, Britain's industries needed all the trade that they could gain in order to pay off the country's huge war loans and to win back worldwide markets from the USA and Japan, which had not been so heavily involved in the war.

As a politician, however, Lloyd George had to please public opinion, and the British people wanted revenge. Lloyd George had just won an election in which the common slogans included 'Hang the Kaiser', 'Make Germany pay' and 'squeeze the German lemon until the pips squeak'. People expected Germany to be punished severely. They also expected the treaty to ensure that Britain once more had the most powerful navy in the world with which to defend her widespread empire.

Wilson

Wilson was horrified by the thought of war. He remembered the horrors of the American Civil War, and had only brought the USA into the Great War as a crusade 'to make the world safe for democracy'.

Wilson now felt that, because it had ignored the chance of peace when it had rejected his fourteen points in 1918, Germany needed to be punished. Yet his main aim was to achieve a treaty that would prevent war in the future, and he still believed in the main principles of his fourteen points:

- that peoples or national groups should be free to govern themselves;
- that a League of Nations should be set up to settle disputes;
- that countries should be open with each other and cut their stores of weapons.

The peace negotiations

All three leaders faced other pressures that had never before affected peace negotiations: journalists, for example, swarmed around Versailles, sending back news to the people of Britain and the USA, as well as France. This put extra pressure on the leading politicians, who had to juggle their own wishes against the need to please their people and to win their votes.

A second, and even greater, pressure on all three leaders was the communist revolution in Russia: they did not want Russia's power to increase and so spread communist ideas. Britain was still sending help to the White Russian army fighting against the communist Red Army. The best way in which to stop or threaten Russia was by means of a powerful country in the centre of Europe, but that country was Germany! If they punished Germany by giving a lot of its land to other countries, there would no longer be a strong enough barrier to hold back Russia. If their punishment made Germany poor, it might also drive the German people towards communism in the hope that it would solve their problems. Indeed, there had already been a communist rising in Berlin in 1919, and communists had won control of Bavaria in southern Germany in April 1919.

The peacemakers' dilemma. A strong Germany was a barrier to Russia, but a threat to France. A weak Germany could not stop the spread of communism, but would not start another war.

QUESTIONS

1 Who were the most important leaders at the peace talks?

2 Why did Germany take no part in the talks?

3 What were the main themes of Wilson's fourteen points?

4 a What were Clemenceau's objectives at the talks?

  b Explain the reasons for his views.

5 a What did the British people want Lloyd George to achieve?

  b Why did Lloyd George wish to be more lenient towards Germany?

6 How did events in Russia cause problems for the peacemakers?

7 You are a journalist as the peace talks are about to begin. Decide whether you are writing for an American, French or British newspaper. Write a report saying what you expect the treaty to say.

Europe before the Treaty of Versailles

N

NORTH
SEA

BALTIC
SEA

GERMANY

Berlin

The Ruhr

SILESIA

FRANCE

The Saar
LORRAINE

Rhineland

ALSACE

AUSTRIA

NORTH

SEA

BRITAIN

RUSSIA

NORTH

ATLANTIC

HOLLAND

GERMANY

BELGIUM

FRANCE

AUSTRIA-
HUNGARY

SWITZERLAND

ITALY

PORTUGAL

SERBIA

SPAIN

TURKEY

MEDITERRANEAN

SEA

0	500	1000 km
0	250	500 miles

Negotiating the treaty: your chance to make history!

What would you have done if you had been at Versailles? Would you have punished Germany harshly or have been lenient? Would you have agree with Clemenceau or with Wilson? Your task is to take the kinds of decision faced by Lloyd George. Before you begin, look back to his objectives on page 17. Make sure that you know what you – and the other leaders – want. You may need to compromise sometimes in order to keep the others happy and to reach a speedy conclusion.

Make a note of your decisions and the reasons for your choice. Later you will find out how well you have done. (Alternatively, work in threes, with each person being one of the 'Big Three', and negotiate among yourselves what decisions you will take.)

NEGOTIATING THE TREATY: YOUR CHANCE TO MAKE HISTORY!

1 Should all the blame for the war be pinned on Germany?
Will you:
a demand that the treaty says that Germany was completely to blame for the war;
b suggest that the treaty does not blame anybody?

2 Should a League of Nations be set up?
Will you:
a agree that a league is vital and join;
b agree to join but only if Germany is also allowed to join;
c say no, because it will limit the freedom of individual countries?

3 Should Germany be split up into smaller countries so that it can never be a danger again?
Will you:
a say no, because Germany needs to be a barrier against Russia;
b say yes?

4 What should happen to Alsace-Lorraine (see map on page 19)? This region was taken from France by Germany in 1870. It is rich in iron ore.
Will you:
a give Alsace-Lorraine back to France;
b allow Germany to keep the region in order to help her economy recover?

5 What should happen to Germany's colonies in Africa and the Pacific?
Will you:
a let Germany keep her colonies;
b give her colonies to other countries, such as Britain;
c put her colonies under the care of the League of Nations?

6 What should happen to the Saar and the Rhineland? The Saar produces 8 per cent of Germany's coal. The Rhineland is the border area between Germany and France.
Will you:
a leave Germany in control of these areas;
b give the land to France;
c look for a compromise – if so, what would you do?

7 What should happen to the German army?
  a Germany should have no army or weapons;
  b there should be no limit to Germany's army. A limit would only increase Germany's anger;
  c Germany's army should be limited to a small number, say 100,000 men.

8 What should happen to the German navy?
  a Germany's navy should be limited to, say, six battleships;
  b Germany should have no battleships at all;
  c There should be no limit to the size of Germany's navy.

9 Should Germany pay reparations (compensation) to other countries?
  Will you:
  a demand that there should be no reparations, because world trade would never recover;
  b demand that there should be reparations, but set at a low amount;
  c demand that there should be a very high payment in order to punish Germany severely?

10 Should Italy be given the lands promised to her by Britain in a secret treaty in 1915?
  Will you:
  a agree to Italy receiving all the lands promised;
  b agree to Italy receiving some lands;
  c tell Orlando, the Italian leader, that this is no longer possible (self-determination for nations is more important)?

11 The Austro-Hungarian empire has already begun to break up. Many different peoples made up the old empire.
  Will you:
  a keep them all in one country, as a barrier against Germany;
  b allow each group to govern itself as a country;
  c put some groups together, to form middling-sized countries?

The Austro-Hungarian empire

Boundary, Austro–Hungarian empire, 1914

0   250   500 km
0   150   300 miles

Negotiating the treaty: what did you decide?

Now that you have made your choices, you must face the consequences. Use the information below to add up the points that you scored, then look at the 'How did you score?' section to see the effects of your decisions.

• • • • • • • NEGOTIATING THE TREATY: WHAT DID YOU DECIDE? • • • • •

1 War guilt
a There is no avoiding this choice. The overwhelming feeling is that Germany is to blame. This clause will justify all the punishments to come. Score 1 point.
b A very brave decision, as you are going against nearly everyone's wishes, and are facing the fierce opposition of Clemenceau. There will be howls of rage at home, and terrible newspaper headlines. Score a brave and politically suicidal 3 points.

2 The League of Nations
a There isn't much choice here. Anything which may stop another war needs support, even if you think that it may be difficult to make a league work in practice. Score 1 point.
b Another brave choice, because few other people want Germany to join. Score 3 points.
c To the other countries, this looks like a very selfish choice. It also suggests that you won't try to stop any country that attacks a neighbour. Score 1 point.

3 Splitting up Germany?
a Yes, the fear of Russia and communism is real, and deciding on how to split up Germany would take ages. You need quicker decisions. Score 2 points.
b It might start another war straightaway, because of the anger in Germany! Score 0 points.

4 Alsace-Lorraine
a France has to get the region back: after all, it was taken away in a war. If you don't agree, Clemenceau may well declare war on Britain! Score 1 point.
b Good for Britain's trade, but it's not a possibility. France won't take no for an answer. Score 3 points.

5 Germany's colonies
a If you let Germany keep her colonies, you miss the chance to increase your own power around the world. People at home will say that you have betrayed your promise to punish Germany. Score 3 points.
b A good way in which to increase your trade, but Wilson simply won't accept this idea. He believes that it is vital for the colonies to decide for themselves who will rule them. Score 0 points.
c It's not what you really wanted, but it's the best that you can negotiate. At least you can now offer to look after some of the colonies – especially the richer ones – on behalf of the league. Score 1 point.

6 The Saar and the Rhineland
a It is not possible to leave Germany in control of these areas, because Clemenceau says that they are a base for future German attacks. If you chose this option, score 3 points.
b This would make Clemenceau happy, but you have just given Germany a good reason to begin the next war. Score 0 points.
c The best solution, but that doesn't mean that it's a good one! There isn't a good solution to this tricky problem. Look at the Datapoint on page 24 to see what was decided. Score 2 points.

7 The German army
a This might be a good way in which to stop another war in the short term, but many Germans will feel that it is too great a punishment. Sooner or later they may try to overturn this decision. Score 0 points.
b This would be one way in which to prevent resentment in Germany, but it is another impossible decision, given the attitude in France. Score 3 points.
c Another compromise, but it's the best you can do, even if you are worried about German reactions. Score 1 point.

8 *The German navy*

a *Another compromise, but it's the best you can do, even if you are worried about German reactions. Score 1 point.*

b *This might be a good way in which to stop another war in the short term, but many Germans will feel that it is too great a punishment. Sooner or later they may try to overturn this decision. Score 0 points.*

c *This would be one way in which to prevent resentment in Germany, but it is another impossible decision, given the attitudes in France and in Britain, where some people hope to take over the German navy. Score 3 points.*

9 *Reparations*

a *You know that this is the best thing to do for Britain's trade. Unfortunately, the British people and the headline writers do not agree: they want Germany to be punished, and you want to be re-elected, so you have to go along with them. If you chose this option, score 3 points.*

b *Even this is impossible, given the demand for punishment. Score 1 point.*

c *This isn't what you want, but it's what you have to accept. Score 0 points.*

10 *Italy's demands*

a *You might go along with this, but Wilson won't agree. He insists on self-determination, even if it means you going back on Britain's word. Score 1 point.*

b *It's worth trying this compromise, but Wilson won't even agree to this. Score 2 points.*

c *This seems the best choice, as it keeps Wilson happy and the USA is far more important than Italy. After all, Italy is no danger to peace in Europe. Score 1 point.*

11 *The Austro-Hungarian empire*

a *Too late for this idea. The old empire has already split up and you couldn't force it back together again. Score 2 points.*

b *Good idea in theory, and Wilson would be happy, but this doesn't provide any security against either future German or Russian aggression. Score 1 point.*

c *Why not? It seems a reasonable answer. It is better than the old empire, so more people will be pleased, if not everyone. Score 2 points.*

HOW DID YOU SCORE?

22 points or more – the higher the number of points, the more you will have done to make sure that there will not be another war, but your popularity at home has fallen rapidly. The people and the papers say that you have betrayed your promise in the election to punish Germany harshly. It seems that your days as prime minister are numbered, but at least President Wilson is happy.

17-21 points – you have compromised as best you could. Maybe everyone is happy. However, there are people saying that you did not do enough to punish Germany. In Germany there is still anger at the treaty. Only time will tell.

16 points and below – the lower the points, the more popular you are at home. You have kept your election promise to punish Germany. You still do not think that this is the best policy, but at least it will win you lots of votes in the next election, and it has kept France happy. Unfortunately, there is great anger and resentment in Germany.

The Treaty of Versailles with Germany

1 Blame
- Germany had to accept total blame for causing the war.

2 Military clauses
- The German army was cut to 100,000 men. Conscription was abolished.
- The German navy was handed over to Britain. Germany could keep six battleships and thirty smaller vessels.
- Germany was not allowed to build tanks, planes or submarines.
- All Germany's wartime weapons were to be destroyed.
- Germany was forbidden to unite with Austria.

3 Colonies
All Germany's colonies were handed over the League of Nations. They were then given to other nations to look after as 'mandates'. The idea was that the mandates would eventually become independent. Germany's African colonies were divided between Britain, France and South Africa. Its Pacific colonies went to Japan.

4 Territory
- Alsace-Lorraine was returned to France.
- The Rhineland (an area 50 km wide) was demilitarised – stripped of soldiers and weapons.
- The Saar was handed over to the League of Nations for fifteen years. After that, there would be a plebiscite (vote) on which country the people wished to live in. During those fifteen years, its coalfields would be used by France.
- Other German lands were given to Belgium and Denmark, after votes on which country the people wished to live in.
- A new country, Poland, was created, mostly from land in the east of Germany.
- Finland, Estonia, Latvia and Lithuania became independent countries.

5 Reparations
Germany was to pay reparations to the allies. In 1921 this was fixed at £6000 million.

Summary of German losses

Land	15%	People	12%
Coal	10%	Iron	48%
Agricultural land	15%	Industry	10%

The other treaties

Austria – Treaty of St Germain, 1919
Austria was forbidden to unite with Germany;
As a result of the treaty, Austria's population fell from 22 to 6.5 million.

Hungary – Treaty of Trianon, 1920
As a result of the treaty, Hungary's population fell from 21 to 7.5 million.

All paid small reparations.
All lost lands.
Austria and Hungary were now separate countries.

Bulgaria – Treaty of Neuilly, 1919
Bulgaria lost land to Greece and Yugoslavia, and its armed forces were limited in size.

Turkey – Treaty of Sèvres, 1920
Turkey's lands in the Middle East were given as League of Nations mandates to:
Britain – Palestine, Jordan, Iraq;
France – Syria, Lebanon.

Self-determination
Two new countries were created in Eastern Europe:
Czechoslovakia – including Czechs and Slovaks;
Yugoslavia – including Croats, Serbs and Slovenes.

After 1919 there were:
3 million Germans in Czechoslovakia;
0.25 million Germans in Italy;
0.4 million Slavs in Italy;
3 million Italians in Romania, Yugoslavia and Czechoslovakia.

Europe c. 1919

ICELAND

N

NORWAY

SWEDEN

FINLAND

NORTH
SEA

EIRE

BRITAIN

DENMARK

ESTONIA

LATVIA

LITHUANIA

EAST
PRUSSIA

Danzig

RUSSIA

NORTH
ATLANTIC

NETHERLANDS

BELGIUM

GERMANY

POLAND

Versailles

CZECHOSLOVAKIA

FRANCE

SWITZERLAND

AUSTRIA

HUNGARY

ROMANIA

PORTUGAL

ITALY

YUGOSLAVIA

BULGARIA

SPAIN

ALBANIA

GREECE

TURKEY

MEDITERRANEAN
SEA

Demilitarised Rhineland

Alsace-Lorraine (French gain)

The Saar

S. Tyrol and Istria (Italian gains)

| 0 | 500 | 1000 km |
| 0 | 250 | 500 miles |

How did Britain react to the Treaty of Versailles?

Political cartoons in newspapers are meant to make us smile – and sometimes to shock us – but they usually also have a serious point to make. If we use cartoons from the past as sources of investigation, they can often tell us something about what people were thinking at the time about an event or an individual. Here are three cartoons from the period of the peace talks. What do they tell us about feelings in Britain?

SOURCE A

DER TAG!

This cartoon was published in *The Daily Express* on 7 May 1919. *Der Tag* means 'The Day' in German, and it was a well-known phrase in Britain, because people believed that German soldiers celebrated 'The Day' when they began their war against Britain. Germany is shown being clutched by a hand.

1 Who are the four figures on the right?
2 What are the feelings of the four figures towards Germany?
3 How do you think the cartoonist felt about the treaty?

SOURCE B

PEACE AND FUTURE CANNON FODDER

The Tiger: "Curious! I seem to hear a child weeping!"

This cartoon by Dyson appeared in *The Daily Herald* on 17 May 1919, after the peace terms had been given to the German leaders.

4 Who does the figure on the left represent?
5 What point is the cartoonist trying to get across?
6 Which cartoon best reflects:
   a the majority of British views about the treaty in 1919;
   b Lloyd George's view of the treaty?
7 Are cartoons valuable evidence about popular reactions to the Treaty of Versailles? Explain the reasons for your answer.

How did the victors feel about the treaty?

In the months after the Treaty of Versailles was signed, all nations took stock of this and of the other treaties. You might expect Britain, France and the USA to have been pleased with it, but there had been too many compromises made in too much haste for this.

The leaders, at Wilson's insistence, had dealt with the League of Nations first. They decided that countries could only join if they gave proof that they would keep international agreements such as the treaty; this meant that the defeated countries were not allowed to join the league. Then the leaders turned to the other issues to be decided by the treaty, but they were short of time and therefore rushed through many decisions that were really too complicated to be rushed.

The question of reparations was the most difficult topic, because it was impossible to decide what Germany should pay compensation for, and also what Germany could afford. Careful arguments were of no interest to many French and British people, or to the newspapers; they wanted revenge, and for Germany to pay as large a sum as possible. Lloyd George knew that Germany could not afford a high sum, and that it was not in Britain's trading interest to fix too high a sum either. But he had to think of the people who had elected him. In 1919 the leaders therefore decided to postpone fixing the total sum to be paid; in 1921 it was settled at £6000 million.

France

Following the Treaty of Versailles, France felt more secure against German aggression, but there was still a strong feeling that the treaty should have been harsher. France had wanted to take over part of the German navy, to have had total control of the Saar, and for the Rhineland to have become independent. Critics of the treaty said that if this had happened, Germany would have been too weak ever to have tried to overturn the treaty. They believed that Germany was still strong enough to seek revenge. This view was summed up by the French general, Marshal Foch, when he said, 'This is not peace, it is an armistice for twenty years'.

Britain

There were two different reactions in Britain. Not surprisingly, after so many deaths, there was much popular support for the harshness of the treaty. Yet some people felt that the treaty would create problems in the future because it was too harsh. Some of the British delegates at Versailles had been heavily influenced by German objections: they asked for last-minute changes, to allow Germany to join the League of Nations and reparations to be reconsidered. Clemenceau and Wilson refused.

> [The treaty is in danger of] reducing Germany to servitude for a generation, of degrading the lives of millions of human beings and of depriving a whole nation of happiness.

These were the words of John Maynard Keynes, the chief British economist at Versailles. He resigned in protest at the treaty, saying that it was impossible for Germany to pay reparations because of her economic problems.

USA

President Wilson was delighted that the League of Nations had been set up. By 1919, however, Wilson's views were less important. He was the leader of the Democratic Party, but elections in 1918 gave his opponents, the Republicans, control of the Senate. Wilson was still president, but the Senate would not agree to his policies. The Republicans wanted the USA to stay out of European politics and, as a result, the USA never signed the treaty.

QUESTIONS

1 List two parts of the treaty that: a) pleased; and b) displeased France.

2 Do you think that Lloyd George was happy with the treaty? Explain the reasons for your answer.

3 The three victors differed in their attitudes. How might this have affected the success of the treaty?

4 You are an MP in the House of Commons. Write a speech giving your views on the treaty and how you see the future of Europe.

How did Germany react to the Treaty of Versailles?

SOURCE A

The *Frankfurter Zeitung*:

UNACCEPTABLE

[the terms] are so nonsensical that no government that signs the treaty will last a fortnight. Germany is crushed.

The *Berliner Tageblatt*:

SHOULD WE ACCEPT THE CONDITIONS, a military furore for revenge will sound in Germany within a few years, and a militant nationalism will engulf all.

The *Deutsche Zeitung*:

VENGEANCE! GERMAN NATION

Today in the Hall of Mirrors, the disgraceful treaty is being signed. Do not forget it. The German people will with unceasing labour press forward to reconquer the place among nations to which it is entitled. Then will come vengeance for the shame of 1919.

SOURCE B

This cartoon was published in Germany on 24 June 1919. The German mother is reassuring her child that 'when we have paid 100,000,000,000 [marks] then I shall be able to give you something to eat'.

SOURCE C

What should we do? … What was the alternative of not signing? Impossible to call the people of Germany to arms for new resistance! The German people definitely wanted peace, were exhausted. Not to sign would mean occupation of the most important territories containing raw materials, intensification of the blockade, unemployment, hunger, the death of thousands, the holding back of our war prisoners – a catastrophe which finally would force us to sign still more humiliating conditions … I finally decided to advocate signing.

From Toni Sender, *The Autobiography of a German Rebel*, 1940.

QUESTIONS

1 How did the newspapers in Source A react to the peace terms?

2 What did they predict would happen in the future?

3 Which part of the Treaty of Versailles does Source B refer to?

4 What is the feeling of the cartoonist about this part of the treaty?

5 According to Source C, why did Germany's leaders sign the treaty?

6 Using all the sources, do you think that the German people were glad that the treaty had been signed? Explain the reasons for your answer.

How did Germany react?

When the peace terms were handed over to the German representatives, they were given fifteen days in which to comment on the detail. Their reply was long and bitter, but it made no difference. Only minor changes were made, and the Germans had no option but to sign. To Germans the peace was a *Diktat* – a peace dictated or forced upon the losers – not a treaty negotiated between equal countries.

The war-guilt clause was the centre of their complaints: it did not seem to make sense, now that the Kaiser, who had led Germany into war, had abdicated. It was the new, democratic government that was being punished for a war that it had not started. Germans also felt that it would be impossible to pay reparations because of the destructive impact of the war on industry, and because Germany had lost so much industrial and farming land as a result of the treaty.

Other clauses also left the Germans feeling bitter and humiliated. Because it was barred from joining the League of Nations, their country was being treated like an outcast. It also seemed that there was one rule for the winners and another for the losers. Wilson's Fourteen Points had asked all countries to cut down on their weapons, but Britain and France did not do so, and they also kept their colonies. Wilson's idea of self-determination caused problems as well. It was a good idea, but impossible to carry out completely: in many regions, national groups lived mixed up together. The plans were furthermore not helped by Wilson's mixture of enthusiasm and ignorance. He gave the South Tyrol to Italy, without knowing that the people who lived there were Austrian; he also did not know that 3 million people in the new country of Czechoslovakia were German. To the Germans, it seemed that all peoples except them had a right to self-determination. One German MP protested: 'The criminal madness of this peace will drain Germany's lifeblood. It is a shameless blow in the face of common sense. It is inflicting the deepest wounds on us Germans as our world lies in wreckage about us'.

How did other countries react?

The outrage of Germany was also felt in Austria, Hungary and Turkey. Both Austria and Hungary had lost over half of their population and also much industrial and farming land. In Turkey, the loss of land to her ancient enemy, Greece, caused a rebellion that toppled the sultan. (see page 38).

Even Italy – one of the victors – felt disappointment. After the loss of half a million lives, Italy expected great gains of land, as was promised by Britain in 1915. Italy did gain land, but not nearly as much as it had hoped. Italy therefore felt cheated by its allies, and its leader, Orlando, walked out when he was told that Italy would not get the lands promised in 1915.

QUESTIONS

1 **Why was Germany not allowed to join the League of Nations?**

2 **Why did Italy's leader walk out of the talks?**

3 **How successfully was the idea of self-determination carried out?**

4 **The text above by a German MP gives you the beginning of a speech. Write the rest of it, expressing your reaction to the treaty and your thoughts about the future. You could also bring in the reactions of other countries to the treaties.**

Germany and the 'stab in the back'

History can be twisted by politicians for their own benefit. As the Treaty of Versailles was being signed, a group of right-wing politicians and generals in Germany was busy spreading its own, different version of recent events. Its alternative version looked something like this.

The German army could have won the war, but it was 'stabbed in the back' by communists and the left-wing politicians who made peace.

The generals called the 'peacemakers' the 'November criminals'.

Then the same peacemaking politicians took over the new republic of Germany and signed the peace treaty. All the problems caused by the treaty were therefore the fault of this group of left-wing politicians.

QUESTIONS

1 Read Source A. Did Hindenburg support this story of the 'stab in the back'?

2 Read Source B. Can you suggest the reasons why this gives a different view from Source A?

3 What can you learn from Sources C, D and E about the reasons for Germany making peace?

4 Why do you agree or disagree with the story of the 'stab in the back'?

5 Write a letter to your local German newspaper telling the truth about these events.

Was the story of the 'stab in the back' true?

S O U R C E   A

In spite of the superiority of the enemy in men and materials, we could have brought the struggle to a favourable conclusion if determined and unanimous co-operation had existed between the army and those at home . . . these circumstances soon led to a breaking-up of our will to conquer . . . As an English general has truly said, 'The German army was stabbed in the back'. It is plain enough on whom the blame lies.

A statement made to a committee of enquiry in 1919 by Field Marshal von Hindenburg, the German commander-in-chief in 1918.

S O U R C E   B

The Supreme Command adheres to its demand made on Sunday 29 September for the immediate despatch of the peace offer to our enemies.

Owing to the breakdown on the [Greek] front, which makes necessary a weakening of our reserves in the west, and because of the impossibility of making good our very heavy losses in the battles of the last few days, there no longer exists any prospect . . . of forcing peace upon our enemies . . . it is imperative to stop fighting in order to spare the German people and its allies further useless sacrifices. Every day costs thousands of brave soldiers' lives.

A letter from Field Marshal von Hindenburg, the German commander-in-chief, to the German chancellor, 2 October 1918.

S O U R C E   C

That is a question of potatoes. We have no more meat. Potatoes cannot be delivered because we are short of 4000 trucks a day. Fat is absolutely unobtainable. The shortage is so great that it is a mystery to me what the people of the north and east of Berlin live on. The workers are more and more inclined to say 'Better a horrible end than an endless horror'.

A description of the situation in Germany by a member of the government, Gustav Scheidemann. Although Scheidemann wanted peace, he refused to sign the Versailles peace treaty in 1919.

S O U R C E   D

General Smuts [of South Africa] came to breakfast on his return from Vienna [in Austria]. There is scarcely any food there and everyone is starving. One of the soldiers gave [a child] a biscuit. Instantly the two men were set upon by a swarm of children, who seemed to come from nowhere, and they were almost torn to pieces as the children fought to get to their pockets to see if there was any more food anywhere.

From the diary of Frances Stevenson, Lloyd George's secretary, 10 April 1919.

S O U R C E   E

Agricultural production in Germany (millions of tons)

	1912–13	1918
Potatoes	52.0	26.4
Rye	11.9	7.2
Oats	9.1	4.3
Wheat	4.9	2.5
Barley	3.6	2.1

Was the Treaty of Versailles fair?

As you can see from the chart, ideas about the Treaty of Versailles have changed over the last eighty years. It is easy for us, with the advantage of hindsight, to condemn the peacemakers for rushing into punishing Germany severely, but we have not lived through the horrors of the Great War. The main difficulty about deciding whether the treaty was fair or not is that each country had a different view. If France had had its way, the treaty would have been even harsher. Germans partly felt that it was unfair because they had been shocked by the end of the war: their government had hidden the news of their country's defeats from them, and many Germans were therefore expecting to win until the very end of the war. They therefore found it difficult to believe that Germany had been beaten. One historian, Sally Marks, has summed up Germany's attitude by saying that the main problem was not that the treaty was very unfair, but that Germany thought that it was more unfair than it was.

Historians' views of the Treaty of Versailles

Many historians condemned the Treaty of Versailles. The treaty was so unfair that Germany was bound to rebel, leading to more conflict.

1920   1955   1990s

The treaty was a reasonable attempt to solve an impossible problem. It was impossible because the atmosphere of 1919 made leniency impossible. It would have been very difficult to do better.

The greatest mistakes made by the peacemakers later became apparent.

- The huge reparations bill hung over Germany for years in the future, impossible to pay off.
- After they had signed the treaty, the leaders of the new German republic (called the Weimar Republic) never had the chance to become popular. It would have been better for the Kaiser and his generals to have ended the war, but Wilson refused to deal with them. As a result, the blame for the German defeat and the treaty was pinned on the leaders of the new Weimar Republic.
- Millions of Germans were left exiled in other countries, angry that they had no right to choose their government or country.
- Overall, the compromises left Germany resentful AND powerful.

QUESTION

1 If you could go back in time to change the Versailles settlement, how would you change it? (See page 24 for details.) Think about whether you would make it more lenient or more harsh, whom you would try to please, and whose views you would ignore.

Summary

World War II was caused by the peace treaty that ended World War I. Many Germans felt that the Treaty of Versailles was very unfair, stripping Germany of land, people and wealth. After that there was bound to be another war, because Germany wanted to restore the balance.

Historian A

Q U E S T I O N S

You have spent some time looking in detail at the treaties that ended the Great War. Look at the chart below.

1 Where would you place your views on the line below?

2 Explain the reasons for your choice.

3 Rewrite the views of the historian above to present your ideas.

The Treaty of Versailles made another war CERTAIN	The Treaty of Versailles made another war PROBABLE	The Treaty of Versailles made another war POSSIBLE	The Treaty of Versailles was not one of the reasons for World War II

5 Did the failure of the league cause World War II?

The League of Nations was created to prevent war. This chapter looks at the following questions:

- why the league failed;
- whether the league's failure was inevitable;
- whether the league's failure was an important cause of World War II.

As you work through this chapter, complete a grid like the one below. During the chapter, you will be asked to add reasons and evidence to the grid.

Reasons for the failure of the League of Nations	Events or other evidence that support your choice of reasons

Source Investigation

SOURCE A

This cartoon was published in the British magazine *Punch* in April 1920. In 1920 a Republican, Warren Harding, was elected president of the United States.

SOURCE B

… the German delegates were brought in, they passed close to me; they looked like prisoners being brought in for sentence … When the signing was finished … the Germans were escorted out again like prisoners who had received their sentences. Nobody got up or took any notice of them, and there was no suggestion that, the peace having been signed, any change of attitude was to be begun …. it was the revenge of France.

An eyewitness account of the signing of the Versailles Treaty by Sir James Headlam-Morley, a member of the British delegation.

QUESTIONS

1 Is Source B a reliable account of attitudes at Versailles?

2 Was the cartoonist who drew Source A sympathetic to the league or to the USA? Explain your choice.

3 What can you learn from Sources A and B about the problems that faced the league?

ASSIGNMENT

There are two major problems faced by the league. You will look at these in more detail later, but this activity is an outline introduction to the problems faced by the league. Your job is to advise the league's Council on how to handle its problems. Tackle each of the problems by following this series of actions:

• Check the Datapoint membership chart (page 36) to see which major countries are members of the league.

• Look at the Datapoint to check which sanctions the league can use.

• Think about the likely consequences of each sanction.

• Decide which course of action to recommend to the league.

QUESTIONS

After each decision your teacher will tell you what action the league actually took.

Either – if you chose the same action as the league, explain the reasons for your choice.

Or – if you chose a different option from the league, explain why you think your choice was better.

Corfu, 1923

Corfu was a Greek island, but its control was disputed by Albania. Italian forces were sent to Corfu to settle this boundary dispute, but a general and several soldiers were shot. In retaliation, the Italian dictator, Mussolini, shelled and occupied Corfu and demanded compensation. Would you recommend the league to:

a enforce economic sanctions against Italy, blocking trade into and out of Italy until Mussolini backs down;

b send in a league army, made up of soldiers from the most powerful nations, to force Italy out of Corfu;

c offer Mussolini a settlement, meeting some of his demands?

Remember!

• Reactions to the slaughter of the Great War;

• Italy had not won as much as expected from the peace treaties;

• countries were trying to rebuild their trade in order to increase their prosperity.

Italy, Corfu and Greece, 1923
[map: Trieste, ROMANIA, YUGOSLAVIA, BULGARIA, ITALY, Rome, Naples, ALBANIA, CORFU, GREECE; N; 0 250 500 km; 0 150 300 miles]

Manchuria, 1931

Japanese forces invaded Manchuria, which was part of China. Japan controlled Korea and had already opened a railway into Manchuria. China was unable to resist because of a civil war, and appealed to the league for help in stopping Japanese aggression. Would you recommend the league to:

a make a statement condemning Japan's actions and calling on Japan to leave Manchuria;

b enforce economic sanctions against Japan, blocking trade into and out of Japan;

c send in a league army, made up of soldiers from the most powerful nations, to force Japan out of Manchuria?

Remember!

• The world has been in economic crisis since 1929. Trade has fallen and unemployment has risen rapidly;

• geography!

Manchuria, China, Japan, 1931
[map: USSR, MONGOLIA, MANCHURIA, CHINA, KOREA, JAPAN; Japanese attacks; 0 500 1000 km; 0 250 500 miles; N]

The League of Nations

The aims of the league

The league was set up to prevent wars by:
- encouraging countries to reduce their numbers of weapons;
- protecting countries from invasion;
- settling disputes over borders.

The membership of the league

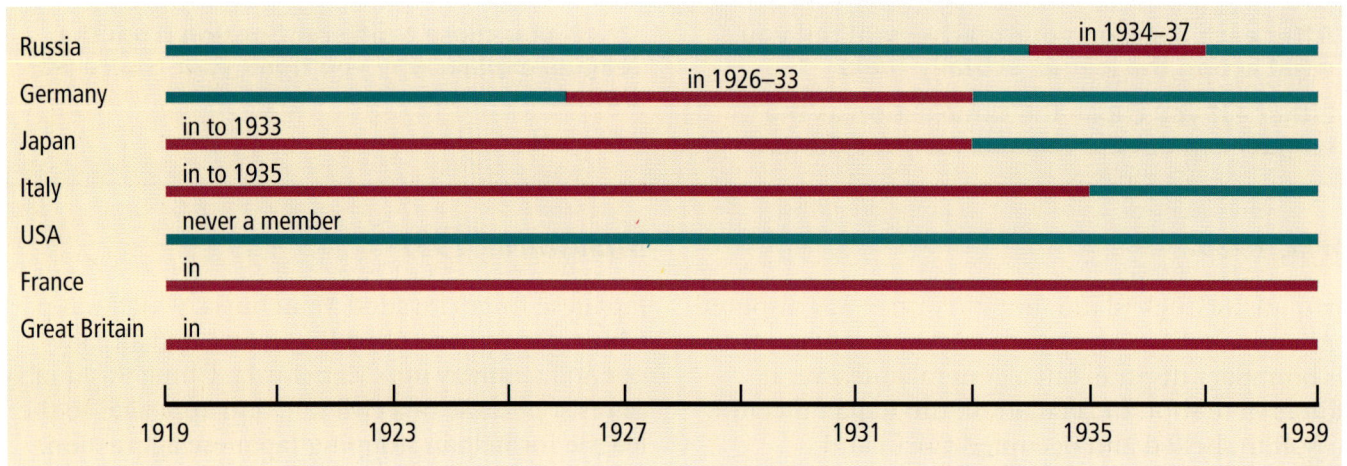

Country	Membership
Russia	in 1934–37
Germany	in 1926–33
Japan	in to 1933
Italy	in to 1935
USA	never a member
France	in
Great Britain	in

Timeline: 1919 1923 1927 1931 1935 1939

Number of member nations
1919 – 41 nations
1924 – 50 nations
1934 – 60 nations

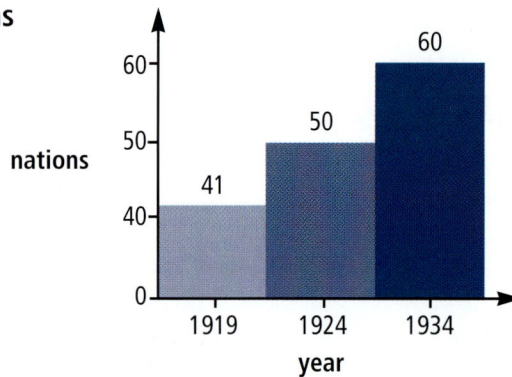

nations: 41 (1919), 50 (1924), 60 (1934)

year

Sanctions – what the league could do

1 Condemn countries that had broken the treaties.

What the league could do

2 Organise economic sanctions against countries that invaded others. Trade with such countries could be banned.

3 Send in a military force to settle disputes. The army could be made up from the armies of different nations.

◄ D A T A P O I N T ►

How was the league organised?

The League of Nations was based in Geneva, Switzerland. It was governed by two bodies.

The Assembly met once a year. Every member country had one vote. Decisions had to be unanimous.

The Council consisted of Britain, France, Japan, Italy plus 4 other countries 1919-26, plus 9 other countries after 1926. Met every 3 months. Dealt with crises.

Permanent Court of Justice based in The Hague, The Netherlands, dealt with legal disputes.

The Secretariat, the league's civil service.

Commissions dealing with special issues:

Mandates Commission ensured that mandates (Germany's old colonies) were properly looked after.

International Labour Organisation tried to spread union rights, improve working conditions and wages.

Refugees Commission helped people made homeless in World War I.

Others tried to produce improvements in communications, health, food supplies, and to work against drug traffic and slavery.

The League of Nations – a report form

Year	Subject	Result
1920	Åland Islands	Settled dispute between Sweden and Finland
1920	Vilna	Gave way to British and French demands that Poland should take over Vilna from Lithuania
1921	Silesia	Successfully divided Silesia between Poland and Germany
1923	Corfu	League ignored by powerful nations. Greece forced to pay compensation to Italy
1925	Greece	Stopped war between Greece and Bulgaria
1931	Manchuria	Unable to stop Japan taking control of Manchuria
1935	Ethiopia	Unable to stop Italy invading Ethiopia or to force Italy to give up its

QUESTIONS

1 Which powerful country never joined the league?

2 Which major countries were members of the league from 1919 to 1939?

3 Why was it important for powerful nations to be members of the league?

4 Do you think that the league would have been likely to use force to tackle problems?

5 Would the league have been likely to take speedy actions to settle disputes?

6 Look at the aims of the league. Do you think that they would be easy, difficult, or impossible to achieve? Explain the reasons for your choice.

7 This chapter has already introduced a number of reasons why the league failed. Complete your grid of reasons for the failure of the league.

Was the league a success between 1919 and 1929?

The two headlines on the right might have been written in 1929. Your task is to decide which was right, and to write an article under that headline for your newspaper. Like any good journalist (or historian), you will need to keep notes of your evidence, so divide a page as shown, and, as you read these pages, note down the evidence for each headline. Then write your article. If you don't think either headline fits the league's record between 1919 and 1929, write another headline and then an article to suit it.

THE LEAGUE: TEN YEARS OF SUCCESS

THE LEAGUE: SMALL SUCCESSES, BIG DEFEATS

Evidence for failure	Evidence for success

1919: The league faces problems. Turkey resents losing lands to Greece and has launched attacks to reclaim those lands. Italy is also very disappointed by the treaties. A breakaway Italian force has occupied the Yugoslavian town of Fiume.

1920: A dispute between Sweden and Finland over the Åland Islands has been peacefully settled by the league. The problem of the region of Vilna (between Poland and Lithuania) is more difficult. Poland seized Vilna while the league was still debating to which country Vilna should belong. Lithuania appealed to the league, but the fate of Vilna has been decided by the Conference of Ambassadors, representing the most powerful nations. Britain and France, motivated by their fear of the spread of communism, decided that Vilna should be Polish, because this would strengthen Poland against Russia. The league has given way to Poland.

1921: The league has successfully organised the division of Silesia between Poland and Germany. Neither side is completely happy, but both are ready to accept the league's decision. The Italian force has left Fiume, but it ignored the wishes of the league for over a year, showing that force can be successful.

1922: The league has settled a dispute between Colombia and Venezuela, two more small countries which are ready to obey it.

1923: The Treaty of Sèvres, dealing with the Turkish empire, has been replaced by the Treaty of Lausanne between Greece and Turkey. Turkey has won back by force the land that was given to Greece by the Treaty of Sèvres. This new, negotiated peace looks as if it will hold. The Greek island of Corfu has been occupied by Italian forces (see page 35). Italy is both a member of the league's Council and the country that is threatening the peace. The league has handed the problem of Corfu to the Conference of Ambassadors, which includes Italy. Greece has been forced to pay compensation to Italy: one of the league's most powerful members has ignored its wishes.

1925: The league has solved two problems: it has ended a dispute between Chile and Peru, and it has prevented a war between Greece and Bulgaria. Greece, which had attacked Bulgaria, obeyed the league's demand to withdraw its army. Germany has signed the Treaty of Locarno, along with France and Britain. The treaty is important because Germany has sworn to maintain its western frontiers with France that were laid down in the Treaty of Versailles. This is very good news for France, but there is no mention in the treaty of Germany's eastern borders. Does this mean that Germany will try to regain land from Poland? The treaty was made without consulting the league. Britain and France do not want to have their actions limited by the league.

1926: Germany has become a member of the League of Nations.

1928: The Kellogg-Briand Pact has been signed by sixty-five countries, including the USA and the USSR, which are still not members of the league. Each country has sworn not to use war to win its arguments, although no sanctions have been agreed against any country that does start a war. The pact was arranged without the involvement of the league; Kellogg was a leading American politician and Briand a French politician.

◄ D A T A P O I N T ►

The Conference of Ambassadors was set up to handle any problems while the league was being set up. It represented Britain, France, Japan and Italy. These countries, however, decided that they had more freedom to make decisions through the conference than through the league, which had many more members. They therefore kept the conference going until 1931.

Look at your grid of reasons for the failure of the league. Can you add any more reasons or evidence to your grid?

How successfully did the league tackle problems in the 1930s?

Ten years had gone by without a major war. Germany had joined the league and, in 1928, over sixty nations had sworn not to go to war as a means of settling their disputes. The next step forward would be disarmament (reducing the number of weapons held by every country). This would make war very unlikely.

There was no progress towards disarmament, however, and from 1929 optimism turned to fear. The first event that damaged the chances of peace was the economic crisis that began in 1929 in the USA, and then spread worldwide. Trade fell catastrophically; people lost their jobs in millions. The result was renewed rivalry between nations, initially over what was left of the world's trade. In Germany, the loss of its rich industrial lands in 1919 was resented even more deeply. France, always sensitive to feelings in Germany, began to build new defences, known as the Maginot Line. In such conditions of economic depression and suspicion, countries were less likely to work together on behalf of the league.

The second problem for the league was the rise of dictators in many countries in Europe: Hitler in Germany, Mussolini in Italy and Franco in Spain. Dictators who had seized power by force were not likely to work with others to prevent war and for the peaceful ideals of the league.

A redrawing of a cartoon originally published in 1925, to show the league's problems around 1930.

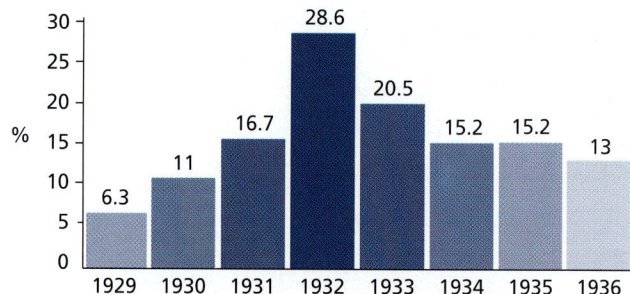

World unemployment

Year	%
1929	6.3
1930	11
1931	16.7
1932	28.6
1933	20.5
1934	15.2
1935	15.2
1936	13

Source Investigation

SOURCE A

The trouble is that there are now more gangsters than policemen.

Benito Mussolini, Italian dictator.

QUESTIONS

1 **What did Mussolini mean by this sentence?**

2 **Name three of the 'gangsters'.**

3 **Which 'policemen' were left in the league by 1936?**

4 **Why did this situation make it more difficult for the league to keep the peace?**

The Manchurian Crisis, 1931

Despite its good results in settling disputes between small countries, the league had not tackled major problems successfully. Its first great test in the 1930s was the Manchurian Crisis of 1931. Japan invaded Manchuria during the Chinese civil war (see the map on page 35); Japan had strong links with the region, but it was officially part of China. Unable to defend her territory, China appealed to the league for help. The league condemned Japan, and ordered it to withdraw its soldiers, but that was all that the league could do.

Britain and France opposed economic sanctions (cutting off trade with Japan), because in a time of high unemployment they were desperate to cling onto all the trade they had. They feared that those countries that did not join a trade boycott would simply replace them as Japan's trading partners, and so the only countries to suffer would be Britain and France. It was also impossible to use force against Japan, for the strongest countries nearest Japan were the USSR and the USA, and neither was a member of the league; Britain and France were far away. Britain also had other reasons for not angering Japan (see Source A). In the end, all that the league could do was condemn Japan for its actions. Japan left the league and carried on with her conquests.

German rearmament

By 1932, it was clear that progress on disarmament was impossible. Sixty countries attended a conference to discuss reducing weapons in 1932, but they could not agree: there was too much distrust. Germany wanted to build up her armed forces again. France would not agree, fearing that Germany would use those forces against her. Germany left the conference. Then, in 1933, Germany left the League of Nations. By 1935, Hitler had reintroduced conscription into the German forces.

Source Investigation

SOURCE A

With Russia and America out of the league, sanctions are a mistake . . . If you enforce an economic boycott, you will have war declared by Japan and she will seize Singapore and Hong Kong and we cannot, as we are placed, stop her. You will get nothing out of Washington but words, big words, but only words.

A letter from Stanley Baldwin, British deputy prime minister, to a colleague, February 1931.

SOURCE B

THE DOORMAT.

A cartoon by David Low, published in the British press in 1932.

QUESTIONS

1 According to Baldwin, what was the USA's attitude to the Manchurian Crisis?

2 Why did Baldwin oppose economic sanctions?

3 What does the cartoonist, David Low (Source B), think of the power of the league?

4 Explain whether you think that this is an accurate or inaccurate view of the league.

Ethiopia, 1935

After the crises over Corfu and Manchuria, Mussolini's attack on Ethiopia (Abyssinia) was not surprising (see the map on the right). Italy already possessed several colonies in the region, and the war helped Mussolini at home. He conscripted 30,000 men into the Italian army. This policy, as well as boosting weapons-producing factories, additionally helped to reduce unemployment.

Ethiopia appealed to the league for help. The league again condemned Italy and introduced some economic sanctions, but did not stop trade in coal, steel or oil. Oil was particularly important: without oil, Mussolini's forces would have ground to a halt.

Why didn't the league stop Mussolini? Everything depended on the attitudes of Britain and France, and neither wished to take action. Britain, with her African colonies and control of the Suez Canal, could have stopped Italy. Britain and France, however, feared that if they tried to stop Mussolini, they would only push him into taking more extreme action: perhaps a European war, or an alliance with Hitler. They hoped that if Mussolini won part of Ethiopia, then he would halt his aggression. They therefore agreed to Italy taking over two-thirds of Ethiopia. The league was completely helpless against Mussolini.

In fact, the result for Britain and France was the worst of both worlds: they had annoyed Mussolini without either stopping him, or making him afraid that they would stop him the next time. Italy left the League of Nations and Mussolini completed his conquest of Ethiopia in 1937. By then he was also allied with Hitler, in what was known as the Rome-Berlin Axis.

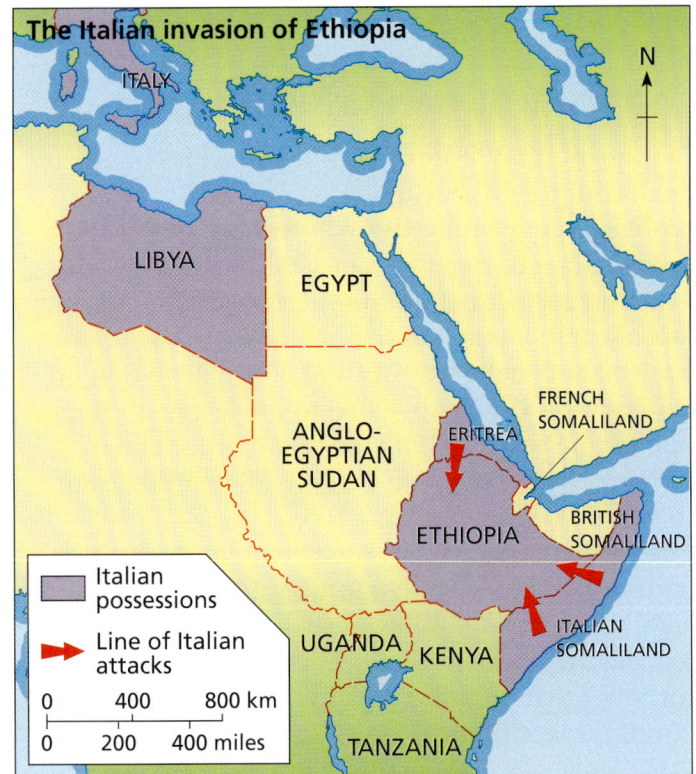

The Italian invasion of Ethiopia

Italian possessions

Line of Italian attacks

Ethiopian troops. Why was Ethiopia so much in need of the league's help?

Benito Mussolini (1883-1945)

Before World War I, Mussolini was a journalist and a socialist. He was very much in favour of the war, however, and therefore split with the Socialist Party and formed his own groups of working-class men to demand revolutionary changes. He was wounded in the war and was angry at the way in which Italy was treated in the peace treaties. His groups of supporters developed into the Fascist Party, and Mussolini became prime minister in 1922 because the king thought that Mussolini could bring order to Italy and prevent a communist revolution. Instead, Mussolini took over from the king of Italy and became Italy's dictator.

Source Investigation

SOURCE A

This is a redrawing of a cartoon published in Italy in 1935. It shows Italy and her children at the bottom right of the picture. Britain is shown at the top left. The caption says 'From what pulpit does the sermon come?'

1 What is Italy's view of Britain?

2 How does this explain Mussolini's invasion of Ethiopia?

SOURCE B

THE AWFUL WARNING.
"WE DON'T WANT YOU TO FIGHT, BUT, BY JINGO, IF YOU DO, WE SHALL PROBABLY ISSUE A JOINT MEMORANDUM SUGGESTING A MILD DISAPPROVAL OF YOU."

This cartoon was published in Britain in 1935.
3 Who are the two figures on the left?

4 Why didn't they stop Italy?

5 What did the cartoonist think of their attitude to the invasion of Ethiopia?

SOURCE C

The league is all right when sparrows quarrel; it fails when eagles fall out.

Benito Mussolini.

6 What did Mussolini mean by this sentence?

7 Give two examples of 'sparrows' and two of 'eagles'.

8 Using Sources B and C, evaluate the power of the League of Nations by 1935.

43

Why did the league fail?

By 1935 it was clear that the league could not stop strong countries from doing whatever they wished. Mussolini was right: the league could deal with the 'sparrows' but not with the 'eagles'. The 'eagles' were too busy with their own concerns, and with their fears for their own safety, to work together for peace.

Was the league's failure inevitable?

Could the league have succeeded? The boxes on one side of the scales show the factors that were working to the league's advantage in 1920. The empty boxes represent those things that tilted the scales against the league.

1 What would you put in the empty boxes?
2 When did the league's failure become certain?

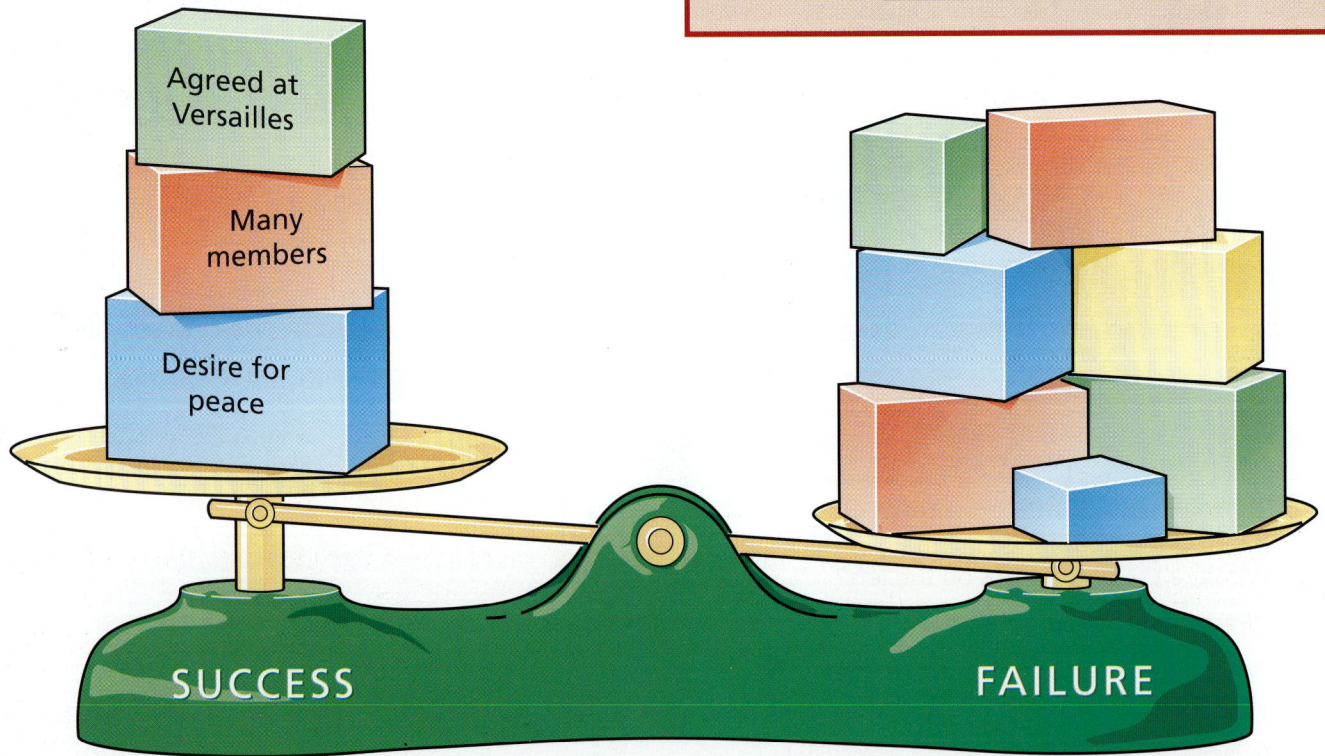

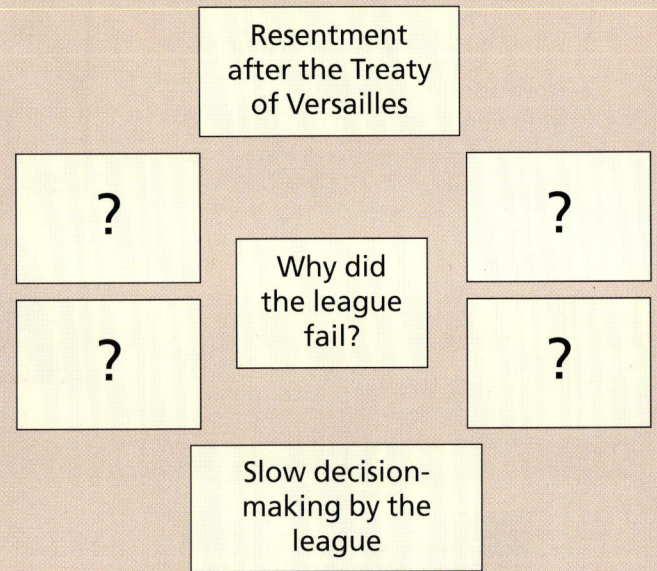

Resentment after the Treaty of Versailles

?

?

Why did the league fail?

?

?

Slow decision-making by the league

Agreed at Versailles

Many members

Desire for peace

SUCCESS

FAILURE

Did the league achieve anything?

Although the league failed to stop another world war, that does not mean that it failed in everything. It may only have stopped wars between small countries, but this meant that many people lived who would otherwise have been killed in those wars. The league reduced pain and sorrow in other ways, too. In 1918 there were many thousands of refugees who had been left homeless by the ravages of war, or by the changes in countries' borders. The league's Refugees Commission was very successful in reuniting them with their families and homes. Its Mandates Commission supervised the way in which Germany's old colonies (known as mandates) were governed by Britain, France and other countries. It ensured that the mandates were governed fairly and that they were prepared for independence.

Other work carried out by the league's commissions was not so dramatic, but was still very important. The Communications and Transit Organisation simplified passport regulations and worked with countries to co-ordinate rail and air services. The International Labour Organisation collected information on wages and working hours, and tried to persuade governments to improve the working conditions of their populations. The Health Organisation carried out important research into diseases, and gave medical aid to developing countries. Other league organisations fought against drug trafficking, for women's rights, and to improve child welfare. Much of this pioneering work was so successful that it was carried on by the United Nations after World War II.

Summary: did the failure of the League of Nations cause World War II?

You have seen this historian before, on page 7, when you first thought about the causes of World War II. After your work on the league, you can now decide whether you agree with this verdict, even though you will develop your ideas further after working on the next chapter.

> World War II could have been prevented if the League of Nations had worked properly. The league was set up to prevent wars, but powerful countries such as the USA and the USSR did not join the league. If the league had been more powerful, it could have stopped German aggression in the 1930s.

Historian B

Source Investigation

SOURCE A

1 When do you think that this cartoon was drawn?
2 What is the cartoonist's message?
3 Do you think that the cartoonist was right?

QUESTIONS

1 How was the league's failure linked to the outbreak of war?
2 Do you think that the league's failure was a) important or b) not important as a cause of the outbreak of war?

6 Did Adolf Hitler cause World War II?

ASSIGNMENT

It is January 1933. In Germany, Adolf Hitler has just been appointed chancellor (prime minister).

You are a journalist based in Berlin, working for an English magazine. Your editor has asked you to write three articles about the new leader of Germany. Here are the headlines that have been suggested:

WHO IS HITLER?

From corporal to chancellor

PEACE OR WAR?

Use the material on the following pages and in any other books that you have to write these three articles. Each section begins with advice from your editor. You should also choose photographs to illustrate your articles and think of captions that will fit them.

◄ DATAPOINT ►

Adolf Hitler

1889 Hitler was born in Austria, the son of a customs official.

1905 He failed his school exams, aged sixteen.

1907 He moved to the Austrian capital, Vienna, where he scraped a living as an artist. When he was due for call-up into the army, he fled to Munich in Germany.

1914 He joined the German army at the beginning of World War I. He was wounded twice and awarded the Iron Cross for bravery.

1919 He joined the tiny German Workers' Party, which later became the Nazi Party.

1923 He tried to seize control of Germany in an armed rising beginning in Munich – the 'Beer Hall' putsch. He failed and was imprisoned for five years but served only nine months. In prison he wrote *Mein Kampf* ('My struggle'), setting out his beliefs.

1932 He stood as a candidate in an election for German president. He was defeated, but won more votes than expected and lots of publicity.

1933 Hitler was appointed German chancellor after his party won the most seats in the election.

Who is Hitler?

Instructions from your editor

People in England know very little about the new leader of Germany. Make your first article a personal one, about Hitler's life and character, so that your readers will be interested and will then be more likely to read your later articles. Some ideas to consider are:

- Was Hitler a leader and a success in his early life?
- How did the war affect him?
- What were his early political aims?
- Did his Nazi Party seem to be heading for success in 1920?

When World War I began, Hitler was just another face in the crowd, celebrating the chance to fight Germany's enemies. Only a few years before, a tramp in a hostel had met 'a man who had nothing on except an old torn pair of trousers – Hitler. His clothes were being cleaned of lice, since for days he had been wandering about without a roof and in a terribly neglected condition'.

The war changed Hitler. He served throughout the war as an ordinary soldier, carrying out the dangerous task of taking messages through the trenches. In October 1918 he was blinded in a gas attack and was therefore in hospital recovering his sight when the war ended. After the war, he stayed in the army, acting as a spy and checking new political groups to see whether they were dangerous to the government. One of those groups was the German Workers' Party. It had fifty-five members and six committee members. Hitler became the seventh.

Hitler soon took over the party. Full of energy, he was the key organiser and speaker. In 1920 he renamed the party the National Socialist German Workers' Party, or Nazi Party for short. By the end of 1920, his party had 3000 members. To them, Hitler issued a twenty-five-point programme setting out his beliefs (Source E).

S O U R C E   A

Munich, 1914. The crowd has just heard that war has begun.

S O U R C E   B

I am not ashamed to admit today that I was carried away by the enthusiasm of the moment and that I sank down on my knees and thanked heaven out of the fullness of my heart for having allowed me to live at such a time.

Hitler's later account of how he felt, standing amidst the crowd in Source A.

S O U R C E   C

No words of mine can describe the satisfaction I felt: within a few days I was wearing that uniform I was not to take off again for nearly six years.

Hitler's description in *Mein Kampf* of how he felt on joining the army.

I tottered and groped my way back to the dormitory, threw myself on my bunk and dug my burning head into my pillow and blanket . . . And so it had all been in vain. In vain all the sacrifices and privations; in vain the hunger and thirst of months which were often endless; in vain the hours in which, with mortal fear clutching at our hearts, we nevertheless did our duty; and in vain the death of two million who died . . . did all this happen only so that a gang of wretched criminals could lay hands on the fatherland?

Hitler's description of his reaction to the news of the end of the war, written in *Mein Kampf*.

1 *We demand the union of all Germans . . .*
2 *We demand equality of rights for the German people with other nations, and the abolition of the Treaty of Versailles.*
3 *We demand land and territory for the nourishment of our people and for settling our surplus population.*
4 *None but those of German blood may be members of the nation. No Jew, therefore, may be a member of the nation.*
11 *We demand the abolition of incomes unearned by work.*
15 *We demand a generous provision for old age.*
18 *We demand ruthless war against all whose activities injure the common interest. Common criminals against the nation must be punished with death.*

Some of the twenty-five points of National Socialism.

QUESTIONS

1 **How did World War I change Hitler's life?**

2 **Does Source A support Hitler's description of his reaction to the start of the war in Source B?**

3 **How did Hitler feel about the end of the war?**

4 **Read Source E.**

a **Which aims would appeal to socialists?**
b **Which aims would appeal to army leaders and other conservatives?**
c **Why was there such a mixture of aims?**

5 **Several sources are taken from Hitler's book, *Mein Kampf*. Is this a useful source for finding out about Hitler's early life and views?**

From corporal to chancellor

Instructions from your editor
This article is more about politics, but it still needs to be interesting: we want people to buy the magazine next week! Some ideas:

• What kind of government did Germany have before Hitler?

• Why was it unpopular?

• How did Hitler organise his campaigns?

• Did Hitler come to power because of his own efforts, or because the earlier governments failed?

The Weimar Republic

Hitler often accused the members of the German government of being the 'November criminals', because they had signed the peace treaty in November 1918. He believed that they had betrayed Germany. This was completely unfair: by making peace, the government (which had just taken over from the Kaiser) had saved Germany from yet more hardship.

The new German government of 1918 was remarkable: instead of being ruled by an emperor, Germany had suddenly become a democracy – a government elected by the votes of all the people. This new democracy had high ideals (see Source F).

The new government was called the Weimar Republic, because the government met in the small town of Weimar. The Weimar Republic faced great problems.

• It was blamed for signing the peace treaty that most Germans hated.

• Germany had serious economic problems. Inflation went out of control in the early 1920s. This problem grew less in 1924, but returned in 1929 as a result of the world economic crisis.

• When the war ended, Germany was plagued by riots and rebellion. The Weimar Republic was attacked by groups of communists and also by conservatives.

• All these problems made the new government seem shaky, which led some to believe that this democracy was not strong enough to lead Germany through her problems to success. This view was not surprising, as Germany had always had a strong ruler, and the army in particular wanted another strong ruler.

S O U R C E   F

1 The German Federation is a republic. Supreme power comes from the people.

20 The members of the Reichstag [parliament] are elected by the equal and secret vote of all men and women over the age of twenty, according to the method of proportional representation.

41 The president is elected by the whole German people.

109 All Germans are equal before the law.

114 Personal freedom is sacred. No one can be deprived of their freedom except through the proper use of the law.

118 Every German is entitled freely to express his opinions by word of mouth, writing, printing or otherwise.

From the Constitution of the Weimar Republic.

S O U R C E   G

Bread prices in Berlin, 1918–23

1918	0.63 marks
1922	163 marks
Jan 1923	250 marks
July 1923	3465 marks
Sept 1923	1,512,000 marks
Nov 1923	201,000,000,000 marks

Bread prices rose so fast in 1923 that people had to be paid twice a day. Workers threw their wages out of the window to their families, who ran to spend the money before the prices went up. As an example, when someone joined a queue, the price of one pound of sugar was 2 million marks. By the time they got to the front of the queue to be served, the price had gone up to 2.5 million.

S O U R C E   H

Unemployment in Germany, 1928–33

Sept 1928	650,000
Sept 1929	1,320,000
Sept 1930	3,000,000
Sept 1931	4,350,000
Sept 1932	5,102,000
Jan 1933	6,100,000

The increase in unemployment in Germany in the years of the world economic crisis.

Extreme left-wing: communists

Extreme right-wing: Fascists e.g. Nazi Party

Weimar Republic

1919–20 Communist revolts in Berlin and Bavaria

1920 Extremists tried to seize power in Berlin

1923 Hitler tried to seize power in Munich

S O U R C E   I

Where he comes from, no one can say. From a prince's palace, perhaps, or a labourer's cottage. But everyone knows: He is the Führer. Everyone cheers him, and he will one day announce himself, he for whom all of us are waiting, full of longing, who feel Germany's present distress deep in our hearts, so that thousands and hundreds of thousands of brains picture him, millions of voices call for him, one single German soul seeks him.

Written in 1922 by a German author, Kurt Hesse.

A failed attempt

Hitler's party had 3000 members by the end of 1920. By 1923, he felt strong enough to try to take over the government by force but, as he and his followers marched through Munich, they met police who opened fire. Hitler was arrested. He was imprisoned for five years, but only served nine months. Between 1925 and 1929 he bided his time. Life in Germany was improving. In 1929, however, inflation and unemployment returned. This was Hitler's chance: one of his colleagues said, 'All that brings about catastrophe is good, very good for us and our German revolution'. In each election, his party built up support, offering simple answers to Germany's complicated problems. The German president tried to avoid appointing Hitler as chancellor but, by 1933, had no choice. Other politicians had tried and failed. Hitler did not have a majority of German support, but he had more than anyone else: he was too powerful to keep out any longer. Even then leading politicians believed that they could control Hitler.

QUESTIONS

1 **Why was the Weimar Republic unpopular?**

2 **Did the reasons for the government's unpopularity change during the 1920s?**

3 **List the methods that Hitler used to win support.**

4 **Why did he decide to use peaceful political methods after 1923?**

5 **How did the Nazis react to the economic crisis in 1929?**

6 **Why did Hitler win support in elections after 1929?**

7 **Was it inevitable that Hitler would become leader of Germany?**

SOURCE P

As I walked through the Berlin streets, the [Nazi] party flag was everywhere. Huge posters and Nazi slogans screamed from windows and shops. Passers-by wore tiny lapel emblems; uniformed men elbowed a way through the crowds, the swastika circling their brawny arms.

Karl Ludecke describing Berlin in 1932 before a big Nazi meeting.

SOURCE O

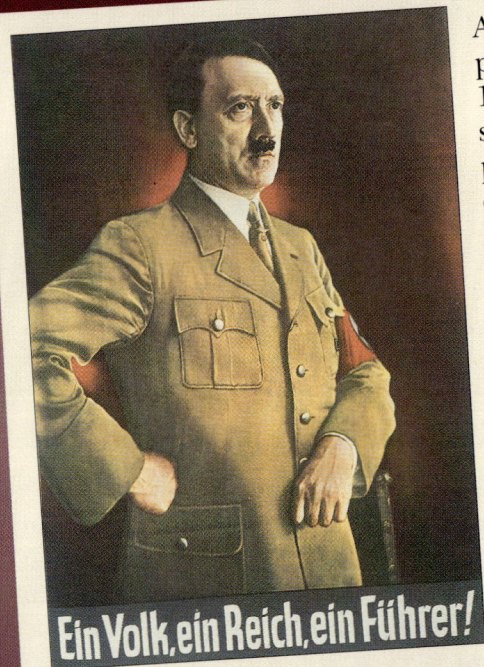

A Nazi electi[on] poster from 1938/39. It says 'One people, one empire, one leader!'

Ein Volk, ein Reich, ein Führer!

Timeline – Germany, 1919–33

Events

- 1919 Treaty of Versailles / Beginning of Weimar Republic
- 1920 Communist and right-wing / Communist risings revolts
- 1921
- 1922
- 1923 Hitler's 'Beer Hall' putsch – attempt to seize power
- 1924
- 1925 Germany joins League of Nations
- 1926
- 1927
- 1928

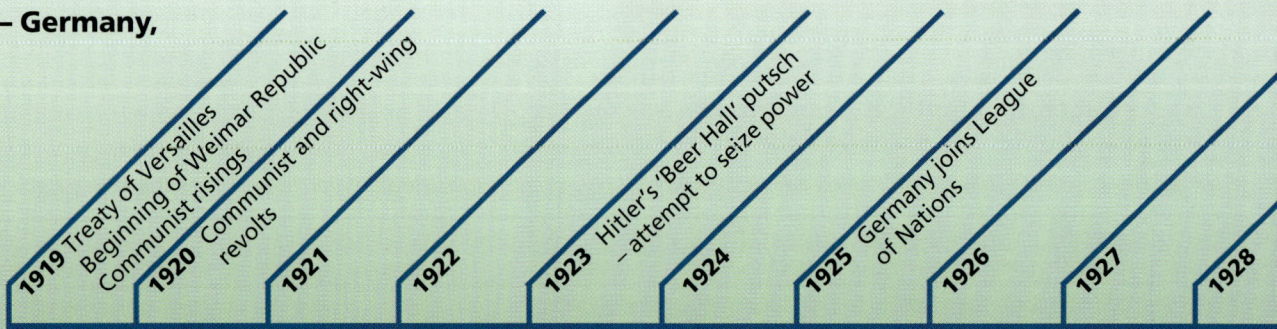

Per cent of votes for Nazi Party in general elections

- 1924: May 6.5% / Dec 3.0%
- 1928: 2.6%

Inflation and high unemployment | Economic improvement

SOURCE J

When I resume active work, it will be necessary to pursue a new policy. Instead of working to achieve power by an armed coup, we will have to hold our noses and enter the Reichstag against the Catholic and Marxist members. If outvoting them takes longer than outshooting them, at least the result will be [lawful].

From a letter written by Hitler in 1923, after he had failed to take over the government by force.

SOURCE K

The understanding of the masses is very limited, and their intelligence is small ... all effective propaganda must be limited to a very few facts and must harp on these in slogans until the very last member of the public understands what you want him to understand ... the first rule of all propaganda is the one-sided attitude it must take to every question.

Hitler, *Mein Kampf*.

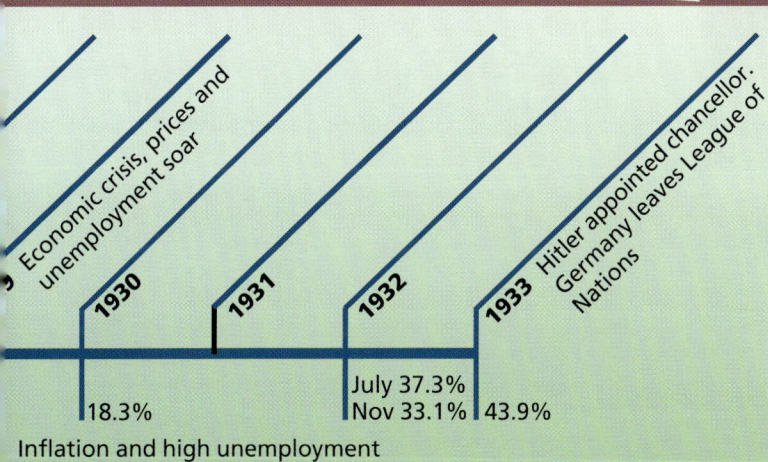

SOURCE L

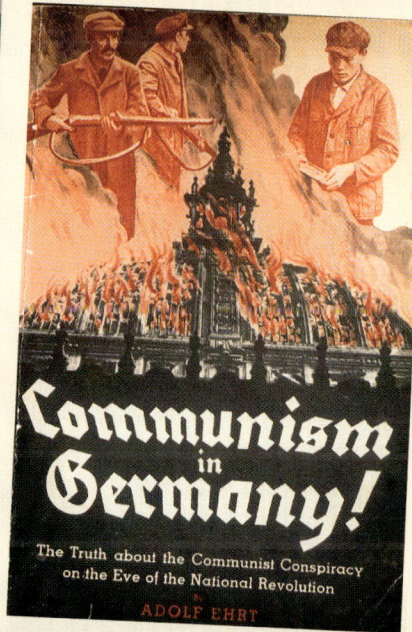

This poster warns of the threat to peace from the communists.

SOURCE N

When [Hitler] spoke of the disgrace of Germany, I felt ready to spring on my enemy ... glancing around I saw that his magnetism was holding these thousands as one ... I was a man of 32, a yearner after the heroic without a hero. The intense will of the man, the passion of his sincerity, seemed to flow from him into me ... I felt sure that no one who heard Hitler that night could doubt that he was a man of destiny. I had given him my heart.

Kurt Ludecke, a leading Nazi, describing the first time he heard Hitler speak at a meeting.

SOURCE M

When our political meetings first started, I made it a point to organise a suitable defence squad ... Some of them had been in the army with me, others were young party members who right from the start had been trained to realise that only terror is capable of smashing terror ... the reputation of our hall guards stamped us as a real fighting force and not just a debating society.

Hitler, *Mein Kampf*.

Economic crisis, prices and unemployment soar
1930 **1931** **1932** **1933** Hitler appointed chancellor. Germany leaves League of Nations

July 37.3%
Nov 33.1%
18.3% 43.9%

Inflation and high unemployment

Peace or war?

Your editor's instructions

People in Britain are still anxious that there will be another war. What they want to know is, 'does Hitler want peace or will he start another war?' You need to answer that question for them, telling them what Hitler has done and said, and whether he seems peaceful. And even if Hitler wants war, does he have the weapons and men to fight one?

Remember, you can use material from earlier in this section.

The rise of the Nazis

The rise of the Nazis

Nazi Party results in German elections

Date	Per cent of votes
May 1924	6.5
Dec 1924	3.0
May 1928	2.6
Sept 1930	18.3
July 1932	37.3 – became the largest party in parliament
Nov 1932	33.1
Mar 1933	43.9

In January 1933 Hitler became chancellor of Germany, but the president, Hindenburg, and other politicians thought that they could control him. Hitler persuaded them to hold another election, saying that he hoped to win enough seats in the Reichstag to gain a majority over all the other parties. That would, he said, make it easier to govern Germany peacefully.

Before the election was held, the Reichstag burned down. Hitler and the Nazis accused the communists of destroying Germany's parliament. A young communist called van der Lubbe was caught in the building, but he may have been a scapegoat. In the outcry that followed, Hitler's stormtroopers arrested 4000 communists and put them in prison without trial. The election was held within a month of the Reichstag fire. The Nazis won more seats, but not enough to give them a majority over everyone else. The Nationalist Party joined with the Nazis, however, and together they voted for the Enabling Law. This said that Hitler could make laws for four years without needing to win votes in the Reichstag. The Enabling Law created a dictatorship in Germany: this was the beginning of Hitler's 'Third Reich', despite the fact that he had never won a majority of the votes in an official election.

The Reichstag fire, 27 February 1933.

SOURCE A

1 We demand the union of all Germans . . . to form a Great Germany.
2 We demand equality of rights for the German people in its dealings with other nations, and the abolition of the Treaty of Versailles.
3 We demand land and territory for the nourishment of our people and for settling our surplus population.

The first three of the twenty-five points of National Socialism announced by Hitler in 1920.

SOURCE B

We stop the endless German movement to the south and west, and turn our gaze towards the land in the east . . . we can primarily have in mind only Russia and her border states . . . England does not want Germany to be a world power, but France does not want Germany to exist at all. Today we are not struggling to achieve a position as a world power, but must fight for the existence of the fatherland, the unity of our people and the daily bread of our children. If we look around for European allies from this point of view, only two states remain, England and Italy.

From Hitler's *Mein Kampf*, 1925.

SOURCE C

Always before God and the world, the stronger has the right to carry through what he wishes. The whole world of nature is a mighty struggle between strength and weakness – an eternal victory of the strong over the weak.

From a speech made by Hitler in 1923.

SOURCE D

On a balcony stood Hitler... gazing at the red ocean of fire. Then he swung towards us. I saw that his face had turned quite scarlet, both with excitement and with the heat . . . Suddenly he started screaming at the top of his voice 'Now we'll show them. Anyone who stands in our way will be shot, mown down. The German people have been soft too long. Every communist official must be shot'.

An eyewitness description of Hitler on the night of the Reichstag fire.

SOURCE E

Germany would be perfectly ready to disband her entire armed forces and destroy the small amount of weapons remaining, if neighbouring countries will do the same . . . But if these countries are not willing to carry out the disarmament to which they are bound by the Treaty of Versailles, Germany must maintain her demand to be equal.

From a speech made by Hitler in 1933. Some months later Germany left the League of Nations' Disarmament Conference.

QUESTIONS

1 Why did votes for the Nazis increase in 1930?

2 How did the Reichstag fire help Hitler?

3 Why was the Enabling Law vital for Hitler?

4 What was the largest vote that the Nazis won?

5 What, according to Source A, were Hitler's main aims in his foreign policy?

6 a Who did he expect to be Germany's main enemies?

 b Why did he expect them to be Germany's enemies?

7 Who did he hope would ally with Germany?

8 Read Source E. What was Hitler demanding at the conference in 1933?

Did Hitler intend to start a world war?

Did Hitler intend to start a world war? This is a difficult question to answer, because we know that he did start a war in 1939. Therefore it's easy to assume that the war started solely because Hitler wanted it to start, and that he had been planning it for several years. What happens in life, however, is not always what people want or plan for and Hitler may – or may not – have intended to start a world war. Here are three different ways of looking at Hitler and at the outbreak of World War II.

1 Hitler wanted war. He mapped out the whole sequence of events carefully in advance. If a war started at one of these stages, then that would be all the better. The strong would overcome the weak.

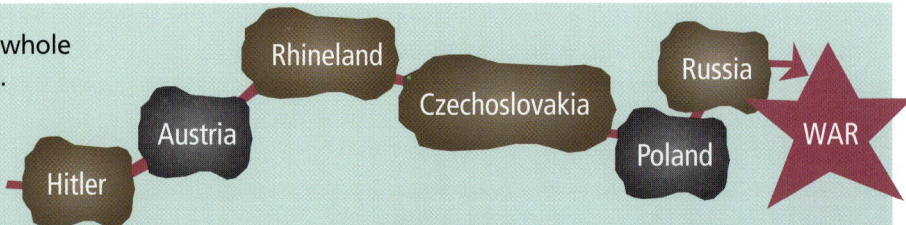

Hitler → Austria → Rhineland → Czechoslovakia → Poland → Russia → WAR

2 Hitler expected war sometime. He intended to achieve his aims, but at the beginning he wasn't sure when or how. Everything would depend on the reactions of other countries. If a war started too soon, before Germany's forces were ready, he would have to step back for a while.

Austria → Rhineland → ? → ? → WAR

3 Hitler didn't want war. He gambled that Britain would not fight another war, and that France would not take action if it was not threatened. He took one step at a time, reacting to events, but he could have been stopped.

? → WAR

Hitler wanted to make Germany into a great country by:

- tearing up the Treaty of Versailles which had taken German land and people, forced Germany to pay reparations and cut her armed forces;
- reuniting all German people – termed the 'master race' by Hitler – in one country;
- giving Germany more living space – *Lebensraum* – to provide more farmland and raw materials such as coal and iron. The space could be gained from the east – the USSR and Poland – the land of 'inferior people' such as Jews and communists.

QUESTIONS

1 Explain Hitler's aims in your own words.

2 Which of these statements do you agree with? Explain the reasons for your choice.
   a Hitler's aims made war inevitable;
   b Hitler's aims made war probable;
   c Despite Hitler's aims, war could have been avoided.

3 From the work you have done so far, which of the theories above seems the most likely?

Hitler's first steps, 1933–36

Rearming Germany

In 1933, a Disarmament Conference met in Geneva to discuss cutting each country's armies and their numbers of weapons. The conference failed because no country trusted its rivals.

Hitler asked Britain and France to cut their weapons to the level that Germany had accepted at Versailles. Britain and France refused. Then Hitler asked if Germany could build up her forces to the same level as that of other countries. Again Britain and France refused. Hitler walked out of the conference (and the League of Nations), claiming that everyone else was being unreasonable.

This was good propaganda for Hitler: he made it sound as though he was only asking for Germany to be treated fairly. In fact, he knew that France would not agree to his demands. He deliberately asked for too much (equality with Britain and France), so that the refusal gave him an excuse to walk out.

Hitler also made good propaganda out of alliances between other countries. As the diagrams show, the countries that were afraid of German aggression had allied together the better to defend themselves in case of attack. Hitler made these alliances sound as if they were threatening Germany.

Hitler began building up Germany's forces and weapons. This policy was clearly against the Treaty of Versailles, but Britain and France did nothing to stop him, for a mixture of reasons. In Britain, ever since 1919 there had been a feeling that Germany had been harshly treated by the peace treaty. Allowing Germany to rebuild her forces was a way of compensating for that harshness. Not only that: other countries were building up their armies and making weapons as a way of beating their employment problems. If Germany did the same, it might even reduce German resentment of Versailles. France responded to Hitler's actions by improving her own defences on the Maginot Line (see map on page 57).

German military spending, 1932–36

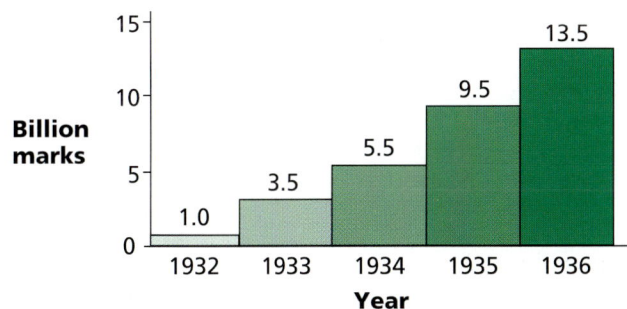

How Germany broke the Treaty of Versailles

Treaty of Versailles	German rearmament
Conscription abolished. Army cut to 100,000	Conscription introduced 1935. 1934 Hitler aimed at army of 300,000. By 1935 he wanted 550,000.
Navy limited to six battleships	1934 Hitler ordered two new battleships.
No planes or submarines to be built	1934 he ordered six submarines. Air force built up by 1935.

1 The French view of the alliances; defensive against Germany

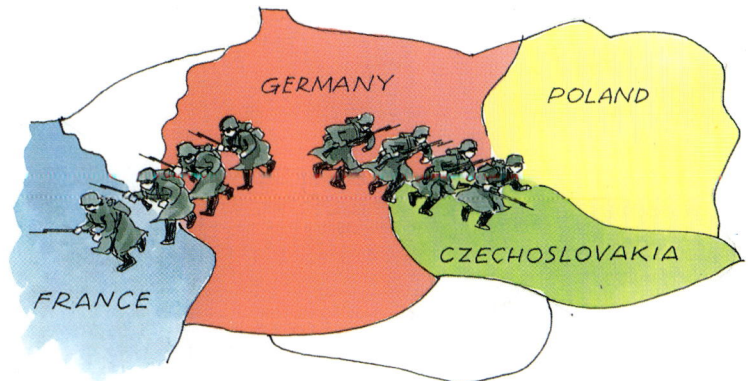

2 The German view of the alliances; aggressive against Germany

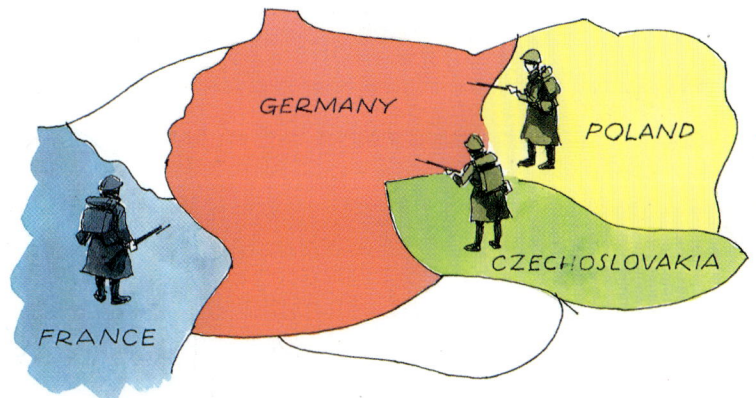

Austria – the first gamble

German rearmament made alarm bells ring in Europe, but at the same time Hitler made a peaceful gesture. In 1934 he agreed with Poland that neither country would attack the other for at least ten years. This was good news, because Germany had greatly resented losing land to Poland at Versailles. Perhaps Germany's anger was fading?

The agreement with Poland meant nothing, however. In the same year, 1934, Hitler tried to take over Austria. He himself was Austrian; there were 7 million Germans in Austria. Hitler believed that Germany and Austria should be one country. There was nothing friendly about his methods, however: he arranged the assassination of the Austrian leader, Dolfuss, by Austrian Nazis. Then the Nazis invited Hitler to take over Austria.

At that point things went wrong. The Italian dictator, Mussolini, did not want a strong Germany on his northern border. He sent troops to the north, threatening to attack the German army if it set foot in Austria. Hitler backed down: he was not yet ready to fight a war.

By 1935 Hitler's position seemed to be worse. Britain, France and Italy met at Stresa, and agreed to stop any further breach of the Versailles Treaty. The duration of this agreement was very brief: the same year, Britain made a naval agreement with Germany, allowing the German navy to grow to 35 per cent of the size of the British navy. This clearly broke the Versailles Treaty. Next, Mussolini invaded Ethiopia. His allies, Britain and France, first condemned him, and then tried to reach an agreement. Mussolini decided that he needed a more reliable ally. Why not that other outcast, Hitler?

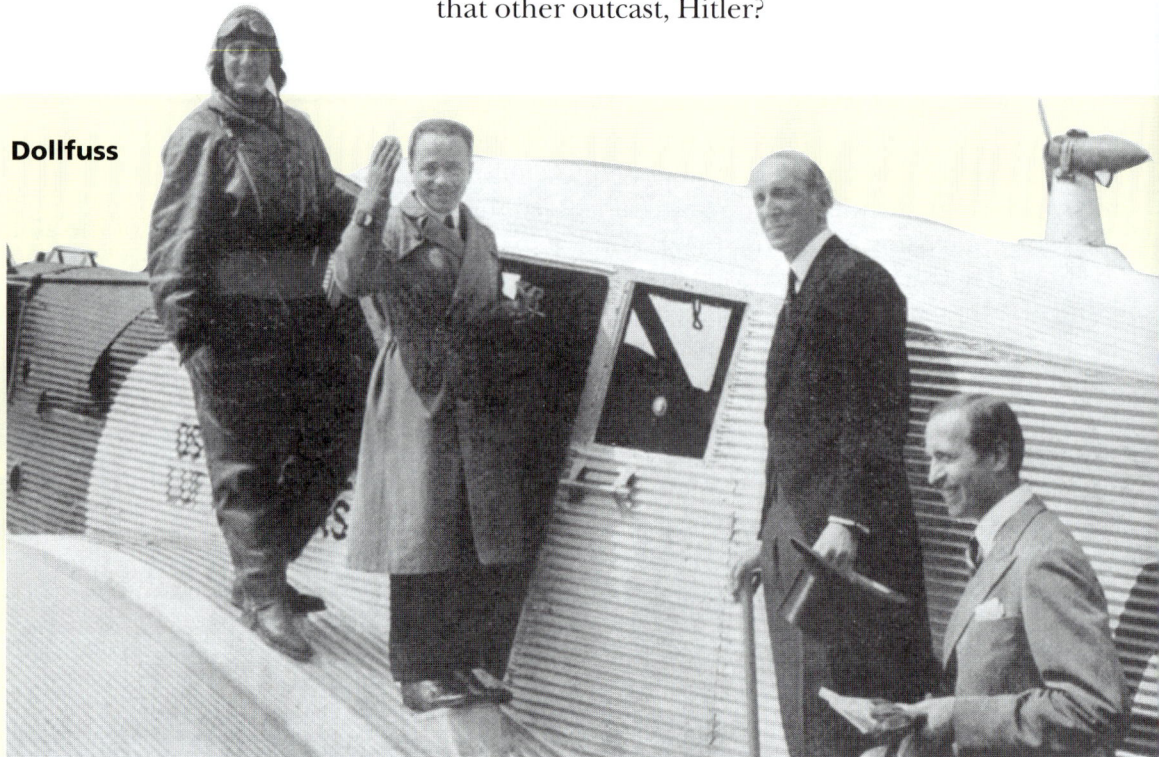

Dollfuss

New alliances from 1935 to 1936

The Stresa Front, 1935

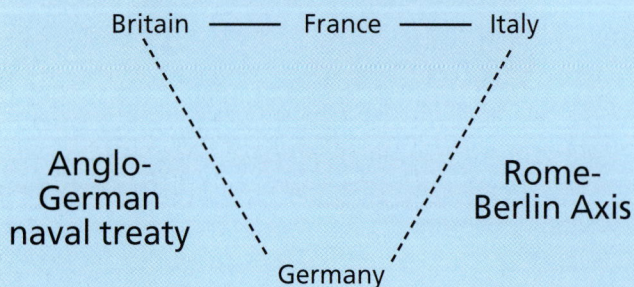

Britain —— France —— Italy

Anglo-German naval treaty

Germany

Rome-Berlin Axis

QUESTIONS

1 How did Hitler make good propaganda from:
   a the 1933 Disarmament Conference;
   b alliances between other countries?

2 Why was Germany allowed to break the Versailles Treaty by building up her forces?

3 Why did Hitler abandon his plans to take over Austria?

4 Was an alliance between Hitler and Mussolini inevitable?

5 How successful had Hitler been by 1935?

Decision 1: the Rhineland, 1936

◀ D A T A P O I N T ▶

The Treaty of Versailles said that Germany was forbidden to have troops in the Rhineland, or to carry out any kind of military activity there. France believed that the Rhineland was vital to its defence, because it was the natural base for a German attack.

What happened?
In March 1936, Hitler ordered a small German force into the Rhineland, reclaiming it for Germany. This broke the Treaty of Versailles. Hitler claimed it was a measure of self-defence, because an agreement made between France and the USSR threatened Germany.

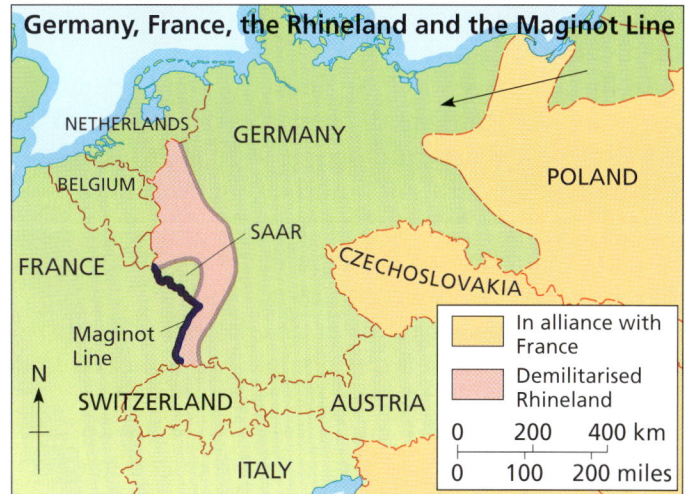

Germany, France, the Rhineland and the Maginot Line

Map showing NETHERLANDS, GERMANY, BELGIUM, SAAR, FRANCE, Maginot Line, SWITZERLAND, AUSTRIA, ITALY, POLAND, CZECHOSLOVAKIA.

Legend:
- In alliance with France
- Demilitarised Rhineland

0   200   400 km
0   100   200 miles

Timeline – events, 1933–36

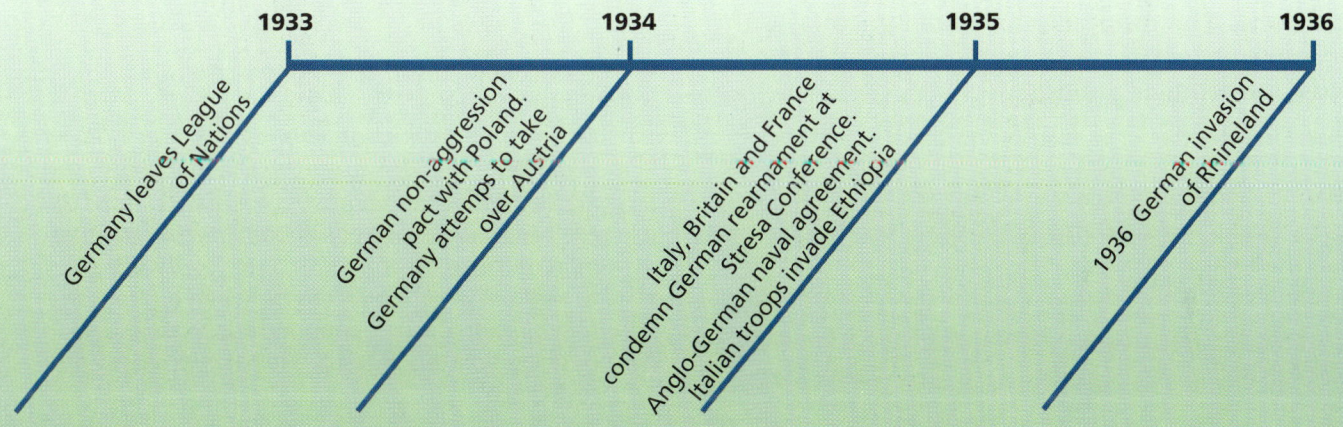

- **1933** Germany leaves League of Nations
- **1934** German non-aggression pact with Poland. Germany attemps to take over Austria
- **1935** Italy, Britain and France condemn German rearmament at Stresa Conference. Anglo-German naval agreement. Italian troops invade Ethiopia
- **1936** 1936 German invasion of Rhineland

A S S I G N M E N T

Your task

You are an adviser to either the British or the French prime minister. You must decide what to advise the prime minister to do.

Your options are to:

1 allow Hitler to take over the Rhineland;

2 ask the League of Nations to condemn Germany;

3 unite with other countries to force Germany out of the Rhineland;

4 send in your own army, regardless of what other countries do.

You need to think about:

- the size of the German forces;

- anxiety about another war;

- the events of the last few years;

- the nationality of the people who live in the Rhineland;

- the consequences of your actions.

Hitler and the Rhineland

Hitler gambled when he sent his soldiers into the Rhineland in 1936: he gambled that Britain and France would not stop him. The reason for sending only a small force was that it was less likely to frighten them into retaliating.

In Britain there was little desire to stop Germany regaining the Rhineland. Memories of the Great War were still very sharp, and people were nervous of anything that might start another war. Another reason was given by a taxi driver to Neville Chamberlain, Britain's foreign secretary: 'Why shouldn't Jerry walk into his own backyard?'

The British prime minister, Stanley Baldwin, also told France, 'if there is one chance in a hundred that war will result . . . I have not the right to involve Britain because we are not in a state to go to war'. During the early 1930s, Britain had reduced her weapons and forces and had not rebuilt them as quickly as Germany. Britain was not ready for war.

France spent more time thinking about sending troops to stop Germany. Yet neither was France ready for war and it would not take action by itself without British help. The result was that Hitler got away with his gamble. After this, as you can see from the chart, he was in a stronger position.

The German infantry enters Cologne in the Rhineland in 1936.

More than once, even during the war, I heard Hitler say, 'The 48 hours after the march into the Rhineland were the most nerve-wracking of my life'. He always added, 'If the French had then marched into the Rhineland, we would have had to withdraw with our tails between our legs, for the military resources at our disposal would have been completely inadequate for even moderate resistance'.

Hitler's interpreter, Paul Schmidt, writing in 1951.

Alliances, 1935

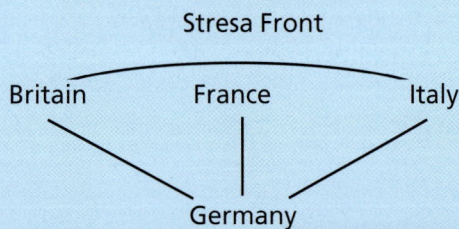

Stresa Front

Britain — France — Italy

Germany

Alliances, 1936

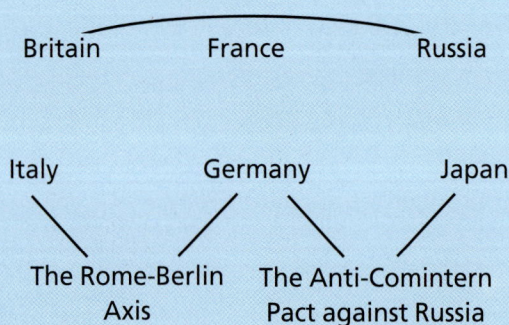

Britain — France — Russia

Italy — Germany — Japan

The Rome-Berlin Axis

The Anti-Comintern Pact against Russia

QUESTIONS

1 Why was Hitler's invasion of the Rhineland a gamble?

2 Why did many Britons not want a war in 1936?

3 Did the invasion mean that Britain and France were more likely to work together in the future?

4 What do you think was Hitler's reaction to not being stopped in 1936?

5 If your earlier decision was different from the actual decision made by France or Britain, explain why you thought differently.

Decision 2: Austria, 1938

◄ D A T A P O I N T ►

The Versailles Treaty said that Germany was forbidden to unite with Austria. It also guaranteed Austrian independence.

What happened?

Encouraged by Hitler, Nazis in Austria began to stir up trouble by means of parades, bombings, setting fire to buildings, and fighting. This forced the Austrian government to ban Nazi meetings, which played into Hitler's hands. He accused the Austrian government of persecuting Nazis, and then threatened the Austrian chancellor, Schuschnigg, with invasion if he did not agree to Hitler's demands. These demands were that Nazis who had been imprisoned should be released, and that the leading Austrian Nazis should be included in the Austrian government. Below is Schuschnigg's account of his meeting with Hitler. If Schuschnigg did not agree, Germany would invade. Schuschnigg tried to gain time by organising a plebiscite (a vote) to see if Austrians wanted to unite with Germany or to remain independent. Hitler would not be put off. He moved his army up to the border, and demanded that Schuschnigg resign and be replaced by a Nazi, Seyss-Inquart. Schuschnigg appealed to France, Britain and Italy for help.

'You, Herr Schuschnigg, have done everything to avoid a friendly policy . . . The German Reich is one of the Great Powers and no one will raise his voice if it settles its border problems … You don't seriously believe you can stop me for half an hour, do you? … Italy? I see eye to eye with Mussolini … England? England will not move one finger for Austria. And France? France could have stopped Germany in the Rhineland, and we would have had to retreat. But now it is too late for France … Think it over, Herr Schuschnigg, think it over well. I can only wait until this afternoon.'

Schuschnigg's account of his meeting with Hitler. He wrote this later from memory.

Armed forces, 1938

	Britain	France	Germany	Italy
Aircraft	1053	1195	1820	1301
Army divisions	2	63	81	73

Germany and Austria c. 1919

A S S I G N M E N T

Your task

You are an adviser to either the British or the French prime minister. You must decide what to advise the prime minister to do.

Your options are to:

1 allow Hitler to take over Austria;

2 ask the League of Nations to condemn Germany;

3 unite with other countries to force Germany out of Austria;

4 send in your own army, regardless of what other countries do.

You need to think about:

• your readiness for war;

• anxiety about another war;

• the events of the last few years;

• existing alliances;

• the consequences of your actions.

The Anschluss – Germany and Austria, 1938

Britain and France did nothing to help Austria. Italy, which had saved Austria in 1934, was now Hitler's ally. Schuschnigg resigned as Austrian chancellor and the leading Nazi, Seyss-Inquart, took over. Then he invited Hitler to send the German army to 'restore order'. Again, Hitler was able to say that he had not invaded another country: he claimed that the German population of Austria had simply invited him to be their ruler. That 'invitation' had horrific results: Hitler's political opponents were arrested; Schuschnigg was sent to a concentration camp, which he survived; many Austrian Jews did not.

Why did Britain and France do nothing? The key was their policy of appeasement. This meant negotiating with Hitler and, if necessary, giving him nearly everything he demanded, in order to avoid another world war. Originally, many people in Britain thought this was only fair after the harsh treatment of Germany at Versailles in 1919. Appeasement was also the result of the British prime minister, Neville Chamberlain's belief that Hitler was a reasonable man. Chamberlain thought that if he negotiated with Hitler, then Hitler would reduce his demands in order to reach an agreement and to avoid war. Chamberlain also knew that Britain's forces were not ready for war.

The Sudetenland, 1938

The Sudetenland was the area of Czechoslovakia that contained the most German-speaking Czechs. Once again, they gave Hitler the perfect excuse for aggression. Czech Nazis were already demanding that the Sudetenland should become independent, but the Czech president, Beneš, was determined to resist them and Hitler. He had made alliances with France and the USSR, in which they had promised to defend Czechoslovakia from attack. The Czechs also had a large, well-equipped army of 2 million men – almost as large as the German army.

QUESTIONS

1 **What was Hitler's excuse for invading Austria?**

2 **Explain in your own words the policy of appeasement.**

3 **What were the reasons for appeasement?**

4 **Why was Czechoslovakia in a good position to resist Hitler?**

Decision 3: Munich, 1938

◄ DATAPOINT ►

The events of 1938

March	German army moved into Austria.
September	Sudeten Germans demanded independence.
September 15	Chamberlain met Hitler at Berchtesgaden. Hitler demanded independence for the Sudeten Germans. If not, there would be war. Britain and France persuaded the Czechs to agree that areas whose German population was more than half, should become part of Germany.
September 22	Chamberlain met Hitler at Bad Godesberg. Hitler increased his demands, insisting on taking all the Sudetenland.
September 29	Chamberlain met Hitler at Munich, together with Mussolini and Daladier of France. The Czech leader was not invited.

ASSIGNMENT

Your task
You are an adviser to the British prime minister. You must decide on what to advise the prime minister to do at his third meeting with Hitler in Munich.

Your options are to:

1 allow Hitler to take over the Sudetenland;
2 unite with other countries to stop Germany;
3 send in your own army regardless of what other countries do;
4 allow Hitler to control the whole of Czechoslovakia.

You need to think about:

• your readiness for war;
• anxiety about another war;
• the events of the last few years;
• existing alliances;
• the prime minister's wishes.

SOURCE A

I am myself a man of peace to the depths of my soul. Armed conflict between nations is a nightmare to me. But if I were convinced that any nation had made up its mind to dominate the world by fear of its force, I should feel it must be resisted.

Neville Chamberlain in 1938.

SOURCE B

I got the impression that here was a man who could be relied upon when he had given his word.

Chamberlain speaking about Hitler after his first meeting at Berchtesgaden.

SOURCE C

Before saying farewell to Herr Hitler … he repeated to me with great earnestness that this was the last of his territorial ambitions in Europe … he wanted to be friends with England.

Chamberlain speaking to the House of Commons on 28 September before flying to Munich.

SOURCE D

Hitler would not deliberately deceive a man he respected … he had now established an influence over Herr Hitler and that the latter trusted him.

Chamberlain speaking to the cabinet after his second meeting with Hitler.

SOURCE E

How horrible, fantastic, incredible it is that we should be digging trenches and trying on gas masks here, because of a quarrel in a far-off country between people of whom we know nothing.

A radio broadcast by Neville Chamberlain on 22 September 1938.

In September 1938, most British people were convinced that another war was about to start. Air-raid shelters were quickly dug and gas masks were distributed to protect people against bombing raids. The government had estimated that 1.8 million people would be killed by German bombs in the first two months of a war.

Germany and Czechoslovakia

How did people react to the Munich agreement?

What happened at Munich?

The four leaders at Munich agreed that Germany should take over the whole of the Sudetenland. They did not discuss this with Beneš, the Czech leader. In return, Hitler promised that he would not threaten anyone else.

This agreement completely weakened Czechoslovakia: it lost important industrial areas to Germany, and disrupted the country's communication system. Poland and Hungary also took over Czech land.

Source Investigation

SOURCE A

Chamberlain emerging from his plane on returning from Munich. In London, Chamberlain announced 'peace with honour . . . I believe it is peace in our time'.

SOURCE B

Give thanks to your God. The wings of peace settle about us and the peoples of Europe. The prayers of the troubled hearts are answered. It was the war that nobody wanted. Nobody in Germany. Nobody in France. Nobody, above all, in Britain, which had no concern whatever with the issues at stake . . . If we must have a victor, let us choose Chamberlain . . . millions of happy homes and hearts are relieved of their burden . . . Now let us get back to our own affairs.

The Daily Express, 30 September 1938.

SOURCE C

I will begin by saying what everybody would like to ignore or forget . . . we have experienced a total defeat. Silent, mournful, abandoned, broken Czechoslovakia disappears into the darkness . . . You will find that sooner or later Czechoslovakia will be swallowed up in the Nazi regime . . . And do not suppose this is the end. This is only the beginning.

Winston Churchill speaking in parliament's debate on the Munich agreement.

QUESTIONS

1 What does Source A tell you about Chamberlain's mood when he returned from Munich?

2 What does Source B tell you about reactions to the Munich agreement?

3 What does Source B tell you about British attitudes to events in Europe?

4 What was Churchill's view of the Munich agreement?

5 Why was Chamberlain so popular when he returned from Munich?

6 Why is it difficult today to understand why Chamberlain was so popular after Munich?

Decision 4: Poland, 1939

Six months after the Munich agreement, the German army invaded the rest of Czechoslovakia. Hitler's next target was Poland. Hitler said in 1939, 'We demand the return to us of the Polish Corridor, which is like a strip of flesh cut from our body. It cuts Germany in two. It is a national wound that bleeds continuously and will continue to bleed until the land is returned to us'.

In August 1939, Germany and the USSR made an agreement not to fight one another. For some time the USSR had been trying to ally with Britain and France, because it was afraid of Hitler's aggression. Neither Britain nor France would ally with the USSR, however, because it was communist. The USSR's leader, Stalin, desperate to avoid war with Germany, chose to make an agreement with Hitler. As well as promising peace, both sides agreed to attack Poland and to divide it between them. This Nazi-Soviet pact meant that Hitler did not have to worry about fighting on two fronts at the same time: in the west with Britain and France, and in the east with the USSR. On 1 September 1939 Hitler invaded Poland.

ASSIGNMENT

Your task

You are an adviser to the British prime minister. You must decide whether to advise the prime minister to declare war.

Your options are to:
1 allow Hitler to take over Poland;
2 declare war.

You need to think about:
- your readiness for war;
- anxiety about another war;
- the events of the last few years;
- existing alliances;
- what the prime minister said about Hitler in 1938.

SOURCE A

[If] any action clearly threatened Polish independence …[Britain] would feel [itself] bound at once to lend the Polish government all support in [its] power.

From Chamberlain's speech in parliament, March 1939.

SOURCE B

Armed forces, 1939

	Britain	France	Germany	Italy
Aircraft	1750	1234	4210	1531
Army divisions	4	86	125	73

SOURCE C

Ciano [the Italian foreign minister] stood up to Hitler very energetically. He has received detailed instructions from Mussolini … to point out to Hitler the madness of embarking on war … He more than once pointed out that a war with Poland would in no way be limited to that country. This time [Britain and France] would certainly declare war … During the meeting next day, Hitler spoke a sentence that still echoes in my ears 'I am unshakably convinced that neither England nor France will embark upon a general war'.

Hitler's interpreter's account of a meeting in August 1939, published in 1951.

The road to war

Hitler invaded Poland on 1 September 1939. He expected to get away with his aggression again. Hitler was wrong: Britain and France did declare war on Germany because of its invasion of Poland. On 3 September 1939, World War II began. It had been just twenty-one years since the end of the 'war to end all wars'.

QUESTIONS

1 Which politician stopped Hitler from invading another country?

2 Choose two alliances made by Hitler. Explain how each one helped him.

3 What excuse did Hitler use for his conquests?

4 Was there one event when Hitler could have been stopped? Explain the reasons for your answer.

5 For each of the events below, explain what the leaders might have been thinking that was different from what they said in public.
   a the Munich Agreement;
   b the Nazi-Soviet Pact.

Timeline, the road to war, 1931–39

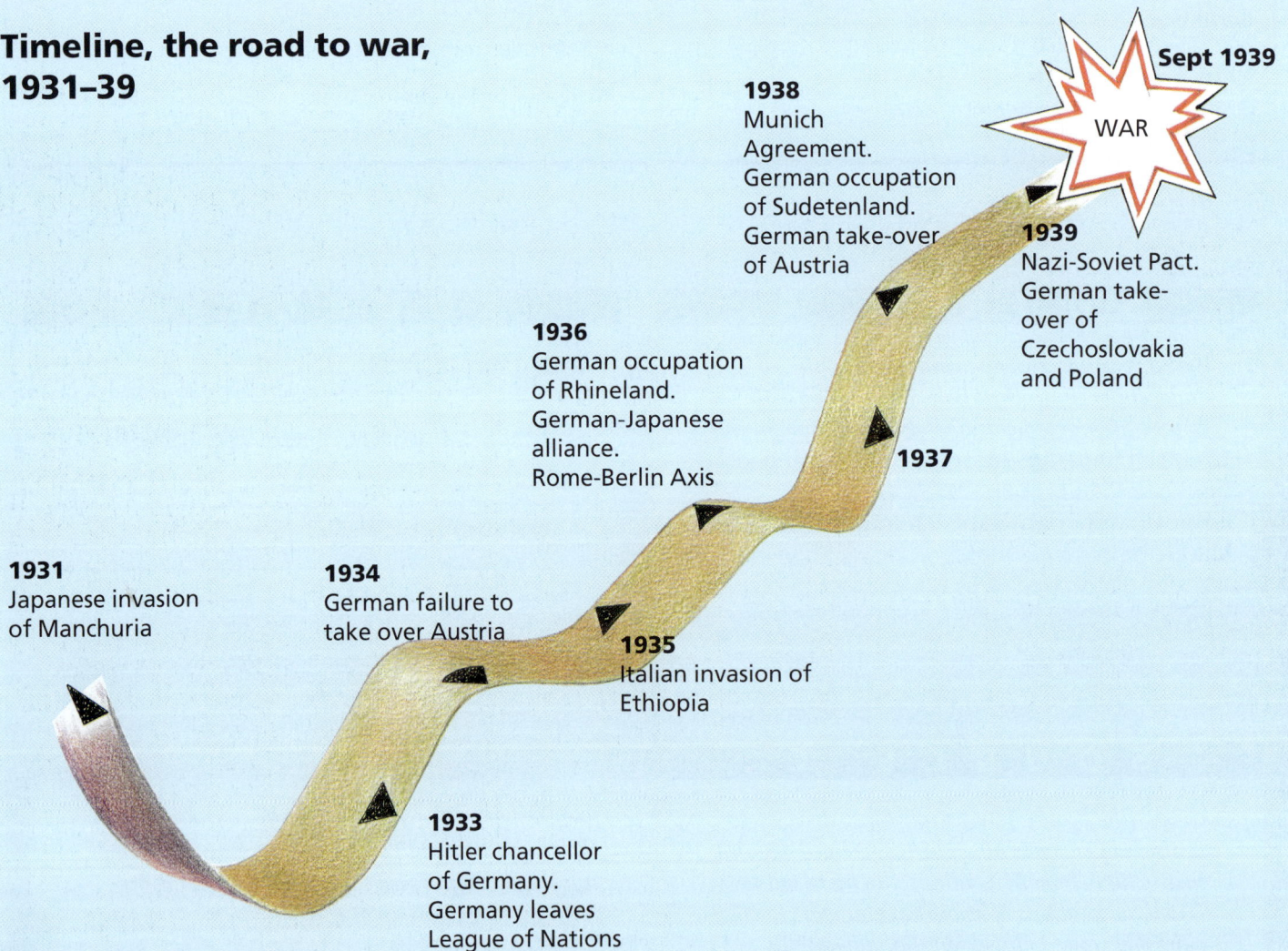

1938
Munich Agreement. German occupation of Sudetenland. German take-over of Austria

Sept 1939
WAR

1939
Nazi-Soviet Pact. German take-over of Czechoslovakia and Poland

1937

1936
German occupation of Rhineland. German-Japanese alliance. Rome-Berlin Axis

1931
Japanese invasion of Manchuria

1934
German failure to take over Austria

1935
Italian invasion of Ethiopia

1933
Hitler chancellor of Germany. Germany leaves League of Nations

Did Hitler intend war?

This section (see page 54) began with three different ideas about whether Hitler planned to go to war. These were that:

1   Hitler wanted war. He mapped out the whole sequence of events carefully in advance. If a war started at one of these stages, then that would be all the better. The strong would inevitably overcome the weak.

2   Hitler expected war sometime. He intended to achieve his aims, but at the beginning he wasn't sure when or how. Everything would depend on the reactions of other countries. If a war started too soon, before Germany's forces were ready, he would have to step back for a while.

3   Hitler didn't want war. He gambled that Britain would not fight another war, and that France would not take action if it was not threatened. He took one step at a time, reacting to events, but he could have been stopped.

ASSIGNMENT

Your work since page 54 has given you a good idea about this question. Draw a chart like the one below and write in each column the evidence that supports each theory. Use the evidence given here and in earlier sections of this book. The timeline opposite will remind you of the main events.

Did Hitler intend war?

Evidence for Theory 1	Evidence for Theory 2	Evidence for Theory 3
Hitler planned everything	Hitler reacted to events	Hitler didn't want war

1   Take each theory in turn. Explain why you agree or disagree with it.
   a   Which theory do you think is most likely to be right?
   b   Which piece of evidence did you find most helpful in reaching this conclusion?
   c   How certain can you be that it is right?

2   Why is it difficult to be certain about Hitler's intentions in the 1930s?

SOURCE A

German and Italian rearmament is proceeding much more rapidly than rearmament can in England. In three years Germany will be ready.

Hitler speaking to the Italian foreign minister, Ciano, in 1936. Ciano was also Mussolini's son-in-law.

SOURCE B

1   *The German army must be ready to fight within four years.*

2   *The German economy must be fit for war within four years.*

A secret message sent by Hitler to his second-in-command, Hermann Goering, in 1936.

SOURCE C

'Do you seriously intend to fight the west?' I asked. Hitler stopped and looked at me. 'What else do you think we're arming for?' he retorted. 'We must proceed step by step so that no one will impede our advance. How to do this I don't know yet. But that it will be done is guaranteed by Britain's lack of firmness and France's internal arguments.'

H Rauschning, writing in 1934. Rauschning was an early member of the Nazi Party who had become one of Hitler's opponents by the late 1930s.

Was appeasement a good policy?

In 1938, nearly everyone in Britain was delighted that war had been avoided. Chamberlain was a hero: his policy of appeasement seemed to have saved Britain and Europe from catastrophe. As soon as Hitler made his next aggressive move, however, it was clear that the policy had failed. Appeasement quickly became a dirty word, linked to cowardice and failure. There has been a lot of controversy about appeasement.

> Appeasement only changed the date when the war began. If Hitler had been stopped in 1936 he would simply have waited until his forces were stronger, and would then have tried again.

> War could have been prevented if Britain and France had stopped Hitler's invasion of the Rhineland in 1936. Hitler had already been stopped once, by Mussolini, when he tried to take over Austria in 1934. Instead, the policy of appeasement only encouraged Hitler to take more. He thought that Britain and France were so desperate to avoid war that they would let him get away with anything.

Historian 1

Historian 2

Historian 3

> Appeasement gave Britain and France the chance to build up their forces. If war had begun in 1938, they might have been quickly beaten.

SOURCE A

We were extraordinarily happy that it had not come to a military operation because . . . we did not have enough strength to attack the frontier fortifications of Czechoslovakia.

General Keitel, one of Hitler's senior generals, speaking after the war about his reaction to the Munich Agreement.

QUESTIONS

1 What were the alternatives to appeasement?

2 Make a list of the reasons why appeasement seemed to be a good policy.

3 Why did the leaders of Britain and France think that appeasement would work?

4 Why did appeasement fail?

5 Appeasement failed. Does that mean that the politicians should not have tried to appease Hitler?

6 Why did appeasement become such a controversial policy?

Why did World War II begin?

In 1918, nearly everyone was desperate to avoid another war. The Treaty of Versailles was intended to take away Germany's strength so that it could not start another war. The League of Nations was set up to prevent disputes from growing into wars. Even in the late 1930s, politicians battled desperately to avoid war. The policy of appeasement tried to prevent war by giving Hitler nearly everything that he wanted. Chamberlain believed that Hitler would be reasonable and would not ask for too much.

World War II began because the German leader, Adolf Hitler, wanted to conquer Europe and create a German empire. Hitler wanted glory for himself and Germany and would not be stopped by anyone.

World War II could have been prevented if the League of Nations had worked properly. The league was set up to prevent wars, but powerful countries such as the USA and the USSR did not join the league. If the league had been more powerful, it could have stopped German aggression in the 1930s.

World War II was caused by the peace treaty that ended World War I. Many Germans felt that the Treaty of Versailles was very unfair, stripping Germany of land, people and wealth. After that there was bound to be another war because Germany wanted to restore the balance.

Historian A   Historian B   Historian C

QUESTIONS

1 Take each theory in turn. Make a list of the events or other evidence that supports each theory.

2 Explain how the main events in these theories are linked.
   a Does the Treaty of Versailles help to explain the failure of the league?
   b Does the Treaty of Versailles help to explain Hitler's actions?

c Does the failure of the league help to explain Hitler's actions?

3 Are there any other factors that help to explain why World War II started?

4 What do you think was the main cause of the war? Explain why you have chosen that factor.

7 The Cold War

Joseph Stalin

During the 1930s, the West saw the Soviet leader, Joseph Stalin, as a brutal dictator. British news-reel films emphasised the misery of the Soviet people under communism. When Germany invaded the Soviet Union (USSR) in the summer of 1941, however, Britain found itself on the same side as Stalin. Stalin's image in the West changed dramatically. In wartime news reels he was now presented as 'Good old Uncle Joe': a kind, fatherly figure; the accompanying commentaries spoke of 'our gallant Russian allies, bravely battling against the Nazi hordes'. The terrible Stalinist purges of the 1930s, in which thousands of Soviets had been sent to death camps, were now conveniently forgotten.

Joseph Stalin in 1935, haranguing a meeting of party activists.

Stalin in approachable mode, congratulating the wives of Red Army commanders.

Who was to blame for the Cold War?

We have just seen that there were two contrasting views of Stalin. Equally, the Cold War itself can be seen from some very different angles.

- The Soviet Union was to blame for the Cold War. Most historians in the 1950s thought that the Soviet Union was largely to blame for the Cold War. They saw the Soviet state as cold and harsh and believed that its aim was to spread the evil communist empire as far as possible.

- The United States was to blame for the Cold War. In the 1960s, many historians decided that it was the USA which was largely to blame for the Cold War. They said that the Americans had not really understood the terrible suffering of the Soviet people during World War II. Americans had not realised that the Soviets were not concerned with expanding their empire, but rather with their own defence.

- Both sides were to blame for the Cold War. Finally, some recent historians have said that both sides carry a share of the blame for the Cold War. They see the Cold War as the result of a mutual lack of trust; each side overreacted. Both sides made things worse by taking an aggressive stance against the other.

In reading through the section which follows, try to look for evidence to support all three viewpoints. Then you can make up your own mind as to who was to blame for the Cold War.

The Grand Alliance

The feeling of support for the Soviet Union grew when America joined the war against Hitler in December 1941; America and Britain were now both allies of the Soviet Union. The wartime friendship and co-operation of America, Britain and the Soviet Union grew so close that it became known as the Grand Alliance. All the differences between the communist dictatorship in the East and the capitalist democracies in the West were put to one side, so that Hitler could be defeated.

The American president, Franklin D Roosevelt, and, to a lesser extent, the British prime minister, Winston Churchill, developed a fairly good relationship with Stalin. They appreciated how much the Soviet people had suffered during the German invasion of the USSR. The Soviet Union had paid a terrible price in defeating Hitler, with a final casualty figure of 20 million people. By the time that the three statesmen met in the winter of 1945, the end of the war was in sight. The question was, would the Grand Alliance survive after the war ended?

Stalin as an ally of the West, with Churchill and Roosevelt

February 1945: the Yalta Conference

In February 1945, the 'Big Three' – Stalin, Roosevelt and Churchill – met in the Soviet resort of Yalta. They knew that Germany's defeat was only a matter of time. News reels showed the three statesmen shaking hands and posing for group photographs. Soviet propaganda films were very positive about the Grand Alliance, but stressed the 'superhuman effort of the Soviet people' and celebrated the 'genius' of Stalin, who had 'cleared out the Nazi hordes'. One historian has called Yalta 'the high point of Allied unity'.

The Grand Alliance; Churchill, Roosevelt and Stalin at the Yalta Conference in February 1945.

Summary

It became clear at Yalta that the Soviet Union and the USA had emerged from World War II as superpowers, whereas Britain was now in decline.

Behind the agreements made at Yalta was a general lack of trust. Churchill was now in a much weaker bargaining position than Roosevelt and Stalin. When Roosevelt spoke privately with Stalin, he tended to criticise Churchill. Stalin trusted no one! Each side also had its own objectives: Stalin was preoccupied with Eastern Europe; Roosevelt was trying to build for the future with the United Nations, and wanted to secure a lasting peace; Churchill was worried that the USSR would take control of Eastern Europe.

More importantly, each had a different idea about how society should be run. Stalin had established a harsh dictatorship, while Roosevelt believed in democracy and capitalism. So perhaps the strange thing about the Grand Alliance is not that it broke up quickly, but that it ever became relatively close in the first place.

Despite the problems, Roosevelt left Yalta happy that the conference had been successful, but complaining that he felt very tired.

◄ D A T A P O I N T ►

The Yalta Conference

Areas of agreement
- The Big Three agreed to set up a new world peacekeeping organisation – the United Nations (UN);
- Stalin reduced his demands for seats in the General Assembly of the United Nations to two or three, rather than the seventeen places that he had originally demanded;
- Stalin agreed that the USSR would enter the war against Japan;
- The Big Three agreed to the division of Germany into different sectors.

Areas of disagreement
- Compensation for the USSR: the USSR had suffered massive losses during the war. Stalin demanded up to £20 million in compensation, but both Britain and America thought that this sum was too high.
- Poland: the Polish question divided the Allies the most. Stalin wanted greater control over Poland, because the USSR had twice been invaded through Poland in the last thirty years. He wanted the new government of Poland to be communist based. Churchill wanted the new Polish

The postwar settlement in Eastern Europe

government to contain some democrats from the government which had ruled Poland before the Nazi invasion of 1939.
- The Soviet Union's ambitions: Churchill was worried that Stalin was planning to dominate Eastern Europe; Roosevelt seemed less concerned. His health was failing, and some historians have claimed that he simply did not have the energy to deal with Stalin's demands.

The alliance begins to break up

Two months after the Yalta Conference, Roosevelt was dead. He did not live to see the end of the war, but when Hitler killed himself in April 1945, Germany was on the brink of total collapse. Allied news reels celebrated the victory of 'Allied might', and the total defeat of 'Hitler's hordes'.

In April 1945, Soviet and American troops came together at the river Elbe in Germany. Their friendliness towards each other was one of the great images of the Grand Alliance.

The defeat of Germany; Soviet troops on the roof of the Reichstag in Berlin.

QUESTIONS

1 Who were the 'Big Three' in February 1945?

2 Using the information you have now read on Yalta, what evidence is there of friendly relations between the Big Three?

3 What reasons can you give to suggest why relations between the Big Three appeared to be good at this time?

4 What evidence is there that, under the surface, relations between the Big Three were based on suspicion and fear rather than on mutual trust?

Roosevelt had been succeeded by President Truman, who was persuaded by his advisers that a new, tougher approach was needed when handling Stalin and the Soviet Union. Truman's opportunity to put this new, tougher policy into practice came when the leaders of the Grand Alliance met at Potsdam in July 1945.

The Potsdam Conference

Although only a few months had lapsed after the apparent friendship of the leaders of the Grand Alliance had been shown at Yalta, the atmosphere and the people at Potsdam were very different. Firstly, Roosevelt's successor, Truman, did not try to build up a relationship with Stalin in the same way that Roosevelt had done. Truman said that 'force is the only things the Russians understand'.

The atomic bomb

While Truman was at Potsdam, he was told that American scientists had successfully tested an atomic bomb, and that it was even more powerful than they had imagined. Churchill noted that Truman was now 'a changed man. He told the Russians just where they got on and off and generally bossed the whole meeting'. A few days later, he told Stalin that America had successfully tested a very powerful new bomb. The fact that the West had kept the new weapon secret from Stalin filled him with fear and distrust.

The Soviets were now determined to speed up their own atomic programme. At a time when the Soviet people desperately needed food, clothing and housing, Stalin decided to invest huge amounts of money in the development of an atomic bomb. Meanwhile, Churchill had lost the general election in Britain, and was replaced by the Labour prime minister, Clement Attlee. This new member of the Big Three shared Truman's view of Stalin. With Roosevelt and Churchill gone, it was becoming clear that the Grand Alliance was breaking up.

Churchill, **Truman** and **Stalin** in front of the Cäcilienhof Palace, the venue for the Potsdam Conference, in August 1945.

The future of Germany

The main issue discussed at Potsdam was what to do about Germany. Germany had been totally devastated by the World War II: one historian described Berlin at this time as being 'a city of corpses, rubble, bombed-out buildings, and broken sewers, wandering women, children and old men – a city of the dead'.

It was agreed at the Potsdam Conference that Germany would be divided up into four zones of occupation (Soviet, American, British and French). Within the Soviet zone in the east, however, was the vitally important city of Berlin. The Allies agreed that this city would be divided into four similar zones, too.

It was also agreed that the USSR would provide food and coal from the Soviet zone in Germany in return for a quarter of the industrial goods that were made in the western zone. The USSR would also be able to take industrial goods from the Soviet zone and send them to the Soviet Union.

Yet, as the Potsdam Conference broke up, it was clear that relations between the superpowers were deteriorating very quickly. Although the new Big Three still smiled for the camera, behind the scenes their relationship had been cool.

QUESTIONS

1 How and why had the leaders who made up the Big Three changed by July 1945?

2 What impact did these changes have on the development of the Cold War?

3 In what ways did the relations of the superpowers deteriorate between Yalta and Potsdam?

4 Which country, if any, would you say was most to blame for the deterioration in superpower relations?

Why did the alliance between the USA and the USSR begin to break down in 1945?

After the Potsdam Conference, the relationship between the USSR and her allies cooled off very quickly. The period known as the Cold War began. The Soviet Union and America soon became deadly enemies: each side regarded the other with great fear and suspicion. Although the extreme tension of the Cold War did not become a shooting war between the two sides, the superpower rivalry between the nations made the world a dangerous place. Both sides built up massive stocks of weapons. On a few occasions, such as during the Cuban Missile Crisis, a nuclear war loomed up as a frightening possibility.

Hiroshima after the dropping of the atomic bomb, August 1945.

Hiroshima and Nagasaki

America's use of the atomic bomb on the Japanese cities of Hiroshima and Nagasaki in August 1945 heightened the fear that was a cause of the Cold War. President Truman called the bomb 'the greatest thing in history', because it had quickly led to the surrender of Japan and the end of World War II. A Soviet propaganda film presented the same event in a very different light, however, showing terrible images of the suffering of Japanese children in Hiroshima, mixed up with pictures of a smiling President Truman at a baseball match. The film accused Truman of taking the decision (to drop the bomb) 'lightly'. This showed how quickly the Grand Alliance was breaking up.

Yet just as Stalin feared the power of the atom bomb, so the West feared the sheer size of the Soviet Union's Red Army. This was why Churchill made his famous 'Iron Curtain' speech in 1946, using chilling imagery with which to emphasise the threat that the Soviet Union posed in its policy of virtual annexation of Eastern European countries.

The Iron Curtain

Although the Red Army had 'liberated' the people of Eastern Europe from Nazi rule, the Nazis were soon replaced by communist-dominated governments. This became a major cause of superpower rivalry. Although Churchill had lost his position as prime minister in 1945, at the start of the Cold War, he still had a major role to play. In March 1946, speaking in America, at Fulton, Missouri, he claimed that: 'From Stettin, in the Baltic, to Trieste in the Adriatic, an iron curtain has descended across the continent'. Churchill told his American audience that one by one the great capital cities of Eastern Europe were falling under the influence of the Soviet Union.

Stalin responded angrily to Churchill's speech: he condemned Churchill's hostile attitude and said that he was setting out to 'unleash war', while the USSR was merely 'anxious for its future safety'. The Soviets criticised the West's 'tendency to forget the colossal sacrifices' made by the Soviet Union, and asked what was wrong with wanting to be surrounded with 'loyal and friendly neighbours'.

How did the USA react to Soviet expansionism?

The Truman Doctrine

The Truman Doctrine was announced in March 1947. In a speech to Congress on 12 March, President Truman emphasised the differences between communism and democracy. One way of life was 'based upon the will of the majority', with 'free elections, guarantees of individual liberty, freedom of speech and religion'. The other was 'based upon the will of a minority . . . it relies upon terror and oppression'. Truman announced that the United States would defend 'free peoples who are resisting attempted subjugation by armed minorities or by outside pressures'.

It was clear that Truman was referring to communism, and that he was now presenting American-Soviet relations as a struggle between the forces of good and evil. Communism was now seen as a threat to American interests and security. The countries that Truman was thinking of when he made his speech were Greece and Turkey. He was worried that mass disturbances there would lead to successful communist uprisings. Greece and Turkey were therefore now to be provided with a massive, American-funded aid programme in order to try to prevent communism taking hold there.

Stalin condemned the Truman Doctrine. He accused the Americans of using 'dollar diplomacy' to extend their capitalist empire.

Marshall aid

After World War II, America had the most powerful economy on earth, and controlled more than half the world's manufacturing production. American propaganda films showed packed supermarkets and cheap cars in order to display the wealth enjoyed by the American people to the rest of the world. In contrast, the Soviet Union was shown in the grip of famine and disease. The choice that the films presented was between communist misery and capitalist prosperity.

The general economic situation of Europe caused President Truman grave concern, however: disease, homelessness and poverty were rife. The Americans feared that the Europeans might turn to communism in desperation.

As a result, the Americans offered economic help to Europe and the Soviet Union to repair the destruction of World War II. Speaking at Harvard University, the American secretary of state, George C Marshall, announced that the United States was ready to provide a massive sum of money to help restore the European economy. He claimed that: 'Our policy is directed not against any country or doctrine, but against hunger, poverty, desperation, and chaos. Its purpose should be the revival of a working economy in the world'. Between 1948 and 1952, the USA injected $13 billion into European recovery by means of the Marshall Plan: Britain received $3000 million, and West Germany $1300 million. American aid included cash, food, machinery and technological assistance. The US provided this partly to prevent West Germany from sliding into economic chaos and thus causing a pro-communist uprising.

The Americans also offered to provide assistance to the Soviet Union and its satellite states. Yet the USSR and Eastern Europe refused point-blank to accept a single cent of American aid. The Soviets felt that America was arrogantly using its wealth to build up its political control, but it may also have been that it would have hurt the Soviet Union's pride to accept American aid. Stalin may have felt that if he accepted aid he would have been admitting that communism was not as effective as capitalism. Finally, Stalin's suspicious character would in any case have made him very reluctant to allow American aid-workers (whom he regarded as potential spies) into the USSR in the way that they had been freely admitted to Western Europe.

In June 1947 the Americans tried 'to put Europe back on its feet' but, in doing so, made the Cold War even worse. The fact was that, even if it was well-intentioned, the Marshall Plan deepened the division between the two superpowers. These events remind us of just how quickly the Grand Alliance had fallen apart. The Cold War had been declared.

Who was more to blame for the Cold War, the USA or the USSR?

This section uses contemporary accounts to look at key moments in the outbreak of the Cold War. Each episode played a part in damaging the relationship between the two superpowers.

SOURCE A

At Potsdam we were faced with an accomplished fact and were … forced to agree to Russian occupation of Eastern Poland. It was a high-handed outrage. Unless Russia is faced with an iron fist and strong language another war is in the making. Only one language do they understand – 'How many divisions have you?' … I'm tired babying the Soviets.

Extract from a letter sent to US Secretary of State Byrnes by President Truman, 5 January 1946.

SOURCE B

A shadow has fallen upon the scenes so lately lighted by the Allied victory. Nobody knows what Soviet Russia … intends to do in the immediate future, or what are the limits, if any, to their expansive … tendencies. From Stettin, in the Baltic, to Trieste, in the Adriatic, an iron curtain has descended across the continent. Behind that line lie all the capitals of the ancient states of Central and Eastern Europe – Warsaw, Berlin, Prague, Vienna, Budapest, Belgrade, Bucharest and Sofia. All these famous cities … are subject to a very high and increasing measure of control from Moscow . . . The communist parties . . . are seeking everywhere to obtain totalitarian control.

Winston Churchill, speaking at Fulton, Missouri, USA, 5 March 1946.

SOURCE C

What is surprising about the fact that the Soviet Union, anxious for its future safety, is trying to ensure that governments loyal in their attitude to the Soviet Union should exist in these countries?

Joseph Stalin, interviewed in *Pravda*, 13 March 1946.

SOURCE D

I believe that it must be the policy of the US to support free peoples who are resisting attempted subjugation of armed minorities or outside pressures.

Extract from a speech made by President Truman to Congress on 12 March 1947.

SOURCE E

Our policy is directed not against any country or doctrine, but against hunger, poverty, desperation, and chaos. Its purpose should be the revival of a working economy in the world so as to permit the emergence of political and social conditions in which free institutions can exist.

US Secretary of State, George C Marshall, speaking at Harvard University on 5 June 1947.

SOURCE F

The US needs to serve the interests of its huge business corporations which are out for world domination. The USA is trying to establish its control over Greece and Turkey by means of dollar diplomacy … Exploiting countries on the pretext of aiding them, under the cover of nonsense about the dangers from communist expansion.

Extract from a Soviet propaganda film made in 1947.

Additional factors that led to the outbreak of the Cold War

- Ever since the Russian Revolution of 1917, Britain and America had been hostile to communism;
- Stalin did not trust the West and regarded each move made by Western countries with great suspicion;
- with the defeat of Germany the reason for the Grand Alliance had gone;
- communism and capitalism were not compatible. Each side believed in a completely different way of life;
- democracy and dictatorship were not compatible;
- both sides were mainly interested in their own 'spheres of influence', rather than in genuinely wanting to co-operate;
- Truman's hard-line approach to Stalin intensified the Cold War;
- America's development of the atomic bomb fuelled the arms race;
- Stalin's disregard of his promises in Eastern Europe, and the expansion of Soviet control there, made it seem that there were no limits to Soviet ambition.

QUESTIONS

Use the evidence you have read to answer the following questions.

1 Imagine you are a historian living in the Soviet Union, and write a brief account of the origins of the Cold War. You should use the material in this chapter to suggest that it was mainly the actions of the United States that caused the Cold War.

2 Repeat the above exercise, but this time suppose you are a historian living in the United States.

3 Try to write an account of the outbreak of the Cold War which has an unbiased, neutral point of view.

◄ DATAPOINT ►

The extension of Soviet control over Eastern Europe

Czechoslovakia Communists won 38% of votes in 1946 elections; communist coup before the 1948 elections led to the resignation of all non-communist ministers.

Yugoslavia Communist government of Marshall Tito elected 1945 and maintained its independence from Moscow; expelled from Cominform in 1948 but remained communist.

Albania Communist republic established 1945, modelled on Russian system.

Poland Communists in control by 1947 and all other political parties banned.

Hungary Communists won less than 20% of vote in 1945 elections, but in control by 1947.

Romania Communists in control by 1947.

Bulgaria Communists in control by 1947.

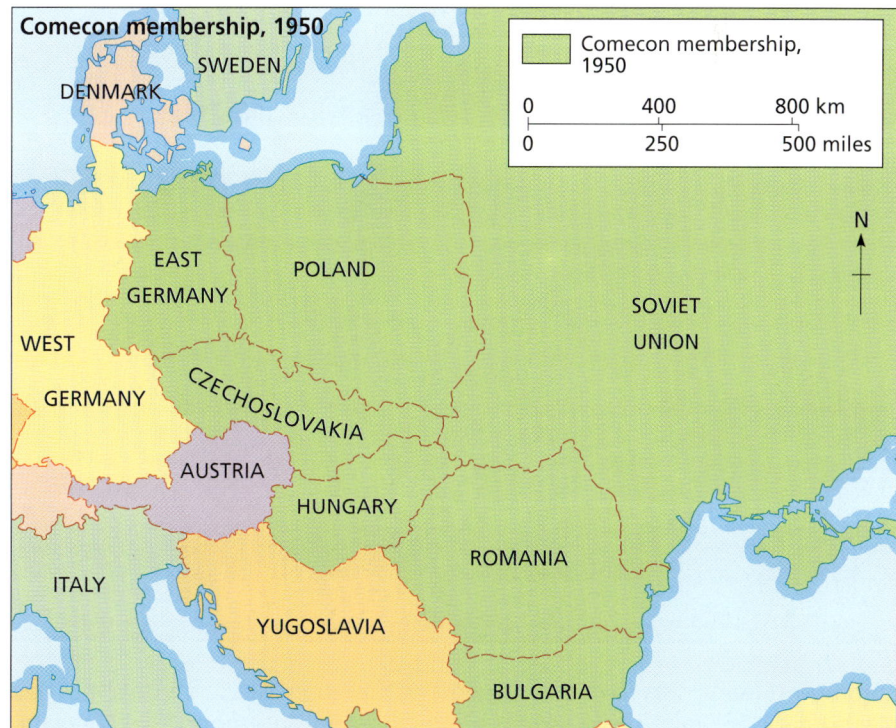
Comecon membership, 1950

How did the USSR control Eastern Europe by 1948?

Stalin's policies

Stalin was determined to protect the USSR from the danger of a future invasion of his country from the West. At Yalta and Potsdam he had tried to ensure that the countries on the USSR's western borders were friendly towards the Soviet Union. Since 1945, the Soviets had installed communist regimes in Poland, Romania, Bulgaria and Hungary. Historian Martin Roberts states that Churchill's warning about the Iron Curtain was proved correct: 'By 1950 a barrier of minefields, walls and fences, patrolled by heavily armed guards and stretching more than 1500 kilometres from the Baltic to the Black Sea had become a reality'.

In any case, Red Army troops were already in place all over Eastern Europe at the time of the conferences. So although Stalin agreed at Yalta to allow free elections in Poland, it would later become clear that there was almost nothing that the Allies could do to enforce this promise. Despite Stalin's assurances, free elections were not being held in Poland, however, and the Soviets also took control of the government in Romania.

Communist leaders from two continents gathered in Moscow's Bolshoi Theatre to pay homage to Stalin on his seventieth birthday in December 1949. They included Mao Tse-tung of China.

How successful was the US policy of containment of the Soviet Union?

Less than twelve months after the Potsdam Conference, the Cold War had begun, and the White House developed a policy of containment. This accepted that there was little that could be done to regain influence over Eastern Europe, which had effectively come under the control of the Soviet Union. The idea of containment was therefore to prevent the Soviet Union from extending its control over any new territory, either in Europe or in the wider world.

The policy of containment was first put to the test in Germany in general, and in Berlin in particular. Then the struggle switched to the Far East.

President Truman in 1946.

The problem of Germany

By the summer of 1946, the agreements made about Germany at the Potsdam Conference were breaking down. The USSR failed to deliver the food and coal which it had agreed to supply from its zone. It also completely stripped its German sector of its industrial resources, and sent it all back to the USSR. One American politician described the USSR as 'a vacuum into which all movable goods would be sucked'. In retaliation, Britain and America ended their deliveries of industrial goods to the Soviet zone.

The Western Allies now decided to make a major effort to boost the economy of their zones. By 1948 the British, French and Americans had merged their zones together in order to make them economically stronger.

Planning the new Dresden, March 1946.

The Berlin Blockade

As tension mounted in Germany, Berlin became the focus of the Cold War. From 1945 this city had been in a unique position: the three western sectors of Berlin were isolated inside the Soviet zone of Germany, more than 100 miles from West Germany. The main road and rail links from West Germany to the western zones of Berlin were therefore of vital importance in maintaining Western contact with the isolated city.

In the summer of 1948, the Soviets began to interfere with the road and rail traffic into Berlin. On 23 June they announced that: 'the Soviet administration is compelled to halt all traffic to and from Berlin from tomorrow at 0600 hours because of technical difficulties'.

The Soviets made this dramatic move because they were becoming more and more aware of the stark contrast between Berlin's prosperous west and poor east. All road, rail and canal routes between Berlin and West Germany were shut down: now they had effectively cut off Berlin from the west. It was estimated that the people of Berlin had only 35 days' worth of food left. The Soviets hoped that the only way in which the West could prevent the West Berliners from starving would be to let West Berlin become part of the Soviet zone. The West would thus lose its only foothold in Eastern Europe, and the division of this area would be complete.

The Allies seemed to have three options:

- to accept the loss of West Berlin and so avoid the risk of a war with the Soviet Union;
- to use force to smash the blockade;
- to launch an airlift to drop supplies into West Berlin.

The West was determined to hold onto its part of Berlin. The Allies feared that if West Berlin was lost, West Germany would probably follow in the same way. They did not want to give into the Soviets, but were also concerned about the danger of war. They decided that the best and safest option was to supply West Berlin from the air, by means of three, narrow, air corridors.

The partition of Germany, 1945

ASSIGNMENT

Working in pairs:

1 Write down what you think are the main advantages and the main disadvantages of each of the three options open to the Allies to beat the Berlin Blockade.

2 Place the three options in what you think is the best order from the point of view of the West in 1948.

3 Which of the three options was actually selected by the Allies, and why?

◄ DATAPOINT ►

The Berlin Blockade

- The blockade lasted from June 1948 to May 1949;
- the first flight, on 26 June 1948, delivered 80 tons of milk, flour and medicine;
- at its peak, planes were landing in West Berlin every three minutes, twenty-four hours a day;
- by spring 1949, the supplies that had been provided were easily enough to prevent starvation;
- Britain provided one-third of the flights, and a quarter of the supplies;
- on 12 May 1949, Stalin lifted the blockade.

A Dakota airlifts essential goods to beat the Berlin Blockade, July 1948.

The Berlin Blockade had ended in humiliation for the Soviets. It was a triumph for the US policy of containment of the Soviet Union, that is, of the idea that the Soviets must not be allowed to extend their empire any further.

Why didn't the Berlin Blockade lead to a war? The main reason was probably that the Soviets were afraid of America's military might. As well as its atomic weapons, the US had moved a number of B-29 heavy bombers, capable of striking targets inside the Soviet Union, to British air bases. Also, the American airlift had helped to avoid a direct military confrontation. Finally, it is likely that both sides realised that an all-out war had potentially disastrous consequences for both sides.

The consequences of the Berlin Blockade

Although the Western allies were pleased with the outcome of the Berlin Blockade, they were also aware of how dangerous the situation had been, and realised the importance of standing together against the Soviet Union. In April 1949 they therefore set up the North Atlantic Treaty Organisation (NATO). The treaty which created NATO was signed by Britain, France, a number of other Western European nations, Canada and most important of all, the United States. The Americans, who were convinced that the Soviet Union was the major threat to world peace, were now making a massive military and political commitment to ensuring the security of Western Europe.

President Truman announces the signing of the NATO agreement in Washington, April 1949.

Source Investigation

SOURCE A

When Berlin falls, Western Germany will be next. If we withdraw our position in Berlin, Europe is threatened ... Communism will be rampant.

General Clay, the American commander in West Berlin, quoted in Fisher, *The Great Power Conflict after 1945* (1985).

SOURCE B

When we refused to be forced out of Berlin, we demonstrated to Europe that we would act when freedom was threatened. This action was a Russian plan to probe the soft spots in the Western Allies' positions.

President Truman, quoted in Fisher, as above.

SOURCE C

The crisis was planned in Washington, behind a smokescreen of anti-Soviet propaganda. In 1948 there was the danger of war. The conduct of the Western powers risked bloody incidents. The self-blockade of the Western powers hit the West Berlin population with harshness. The people were freezing and starving. In the spring of 1949 the USA was forced to yield ... their war plans had come to nothing, because of the conduct of the Soviet Union.

The Soviet viewpoint, quoted in Fisher, as above.

QUESTION

Which view of the Berlin Blockade would you agree with: Source B or Source C? Explain your reasons.

The spread of communism

If America was feeling complacent after the success of the Berlin Blockade and the signing of the NATO agreement, it was shaken to the core by two developments in 1949. Firstly, in the autumn, American scientists detected signs that the Soviet Union had successfully tested an atomic device. This was a disaster for the Americans, who had assumed that it would take the Soviets much longer to reach this stage. The Americans were already worried about the massive build-up of conventional weapons, soldiers and tanks that the Soviet Union was carrying out. So disturbed were the Americans, that the famous magazine *Newsweek* asked with alarm, 'Could the US lick Red Russia?'

Many Americans now expected their country to take a firm stand against what they saw as the rapid expansion of communism. American policy in the Far East rested on the prospect of a close relationship between the United States and China. The White House hoped that the outcome of the Chinese civil war would be a victory for the nationalist leader, Chiang Kai-shek, at the expense of the communist leader, Mao Tse-tung. However, by 1949 the tide had turned in favour of the communists, and by October of that year Mao Tse-tung had taken complete control of the most populous nation on earth, much to the alarm of the anti-communist Americans.

In America, the fear of communist expansion reached a new pitch. Many Americans said that although the policy of containment had been successful in Europe, it was now under threat in the Far East. The future of Japan was now of grave concern to America. It was against this background that the Korean War took place.

Mao Tse-tung, who became leader of China in 1949, pictured in 1934.

9 The Korean War

Korea: the background

Korea is a relatively small peninsula, divided in the middle by a line that is known as the '38th Parallel'. Today, there is a communist government in the north and a non-communist regime in the south. Korea has two very powerful neighbours: to the north it is bordered by China, and off its southern coast are the islands which make up Japan. Known as 'The Land of the Morning Calm', Korea became the centre of one of the most bitter and bloody wars of the twentieth century.

The war started on 25 June 1950, when the communists of North Korea crossed the 38th Parallel and invaded the non-communist south. The war ended with an armistice that was signed at Panmunjom on 27 July 1953. The armistice left both sides where they had been before the war started.

US/UN troops on 'T-bone hill', under communist attack during the Korean War in 1952.

The Korean War 1950

0 — 200 km
0 — 100 miles

CHINA
Yalu R.
Chinese intervention Oct 1950
UN maximum advance 24 Nov 1950
US task force
NORTH KOREA
Pyongyang
N
Inchon
Seoul
Sea of Japan
US landings, 15 Sept 1950
SOUTH KOREA
North Korean maximum advance, 15 Sept 1950
Yellow Sea
Pusan
UN military supplies

The Korean War 1951

0 — 200 km
0 — 100 miles

CHINA
Yalu R.
NORTH KOREA
Pyongyang
N
Inchon
Seoul
Sea of Japan
Chinese and North Korean maximum advance, 25 Jan 1951
SOUTH KOREA
Yellow Sea
Pusan

The Korean War 1953

0 — 200 km
0 — 100 miles

CHINA
Yalu R.
Pyongyang
N
Armistice line, 27 July 1953
Inchon
Seoul
Sea of Japan
SOUTH KOREA
Yellow Sea
Pusan

The origins of the Korean War

Korea had been controlled by Japan since 1910. In 1945, the defeated Japanese forces surrendered to the USSR in the north of Korea, and to American forces in the south. A temporary dividing line was drawn up along the 38th Parallel. The plan was that Korea should later hold free elections and be reunited. Even after the troops withdrew, however, the north remained under the influence of communism, and the south was being backed by America. In 1948, two separate countries were created: the communist North Korea, with its capital at Pyongyang, was led by Kim Il Sung; the non-communist South Korea, with its capital at Seoul, was led by Syngman Rhee.

Anti-American propaganda produced in Korea during the Korean War.

June – July 1950

On 25 June 1950, thousands of communist troops from North Korea, armed with Soviet-made weapons, poured over the border into South Korea.

As the communists crossed the 38th Parallel, they met little resistance. Within three days, the South Korean capital, Seoul, had been captured by the communists. The south was unprepared for the invasion, and was quickly overrun by the North Korean troops. The fate of the south now rested on the need for outside help.

The role of the United Nations in the Korean War

Although Mao Tse-tung had taken control of China in 1949, the United Nations refused to recognise the new communist regime. The USSR was angered by this anti-communist decision, and refused to attend the meetings of the United Nation's Security Council. In the Soviet Union's absence, the Security Council passed an American resolution calling for the withdrawal of North Korean forces to above the 38th Parallel. If the Soviets had not been boycotting the Security Council meeting, they would quite certainly have used their veto to block the American-sponsored proposal.

The UN's objective was 'to furnish such assistance to the Republic of Korea as may be necessary to repel the armed attack and to restore peace and security in the area'. The UN called for its members to offer assistance to South Korea; America was the first country to do so.

American soldiers marching towards the front pass a column of South Korean refugees.

Why did America get involved ?

America regarded the loss of China to communism as a disaster. Although its policy of containment had worked in the case of the Berlin Blockade, America had looked on with dismay as the communists had triumphed in China. President Truman was blamed for not stepping in to intervene: it was said that he was going 'soft on communism'.

The USSR had welcomed the communist victory in China, and many Americans now felt that the Soviets were behind the communist invasion of South Korea. It was feared that if the Americans did not stand up to this communist aggression, then eventually the USSR would take control of Japan. Only two days after the invasion, President Truman therefore gave orders for American troops to defend South Korea. They would not serve as American soldiers, however, but as members of the UN.

July 1950

The American general, Douglas MacArthur, was named as supreme UN commander. Although the majority of the soldiers who served in Korea were American, all of the troops served under the United Nations' flag. In total, sixteen nations sent troops to Korea, and five others supplied medical units. The Soviet Union and China declared that the UN's action was illegal.

Ground forces arrived in Korea on 4 July, but by the time that the majority of the UN forces had arrived, North Korea had succeeded in occupying almost all of the south.

August – September 1950

The Soviets resumed their place on the Security Council in August 1950. Meanwhile, MacArthur's forces had only been able to occupy a small area of South Korea, around the south-eastern port of Pusan. Then, on 15 September, they launched a bold, amphibious landing at Inchon, in the far north of South Korea. This placed the UN troops far behind the North Korean lines. For the first time, the communists had been out-manoeuvred: MacArthur's brilliant strategy had enabled the UN forces to push the communists back towards the 38th Parallel. By the end of the month, General MacArthur was able to retake Seoul.

General MacArthur (pointing, left) in Korea with other US officers after the Inchon landing.

October – November 1950: China enters the Korean War

On 1 October 1950, South Korean troops moved across the 38th Parallel into North Korea. It was now clear that the UN troops had gone beyond their original mission of restoring independence to South Korea: forces under US command were now moving into North Korea. Encouraged by his initial success, General MacArthur had seen the possibility of uniting the whole country and of freeing the north from communist control. By the end of October, the first troops of MacArthur's mainly American army were close to the Yalu river, which was the border between North Korea and China.

As the UN troops moved north, China condemned their action. China felt threatened: perhaps the UN soldiers might use their success in the north to launch an attack on China itself. Mao Tse-tung warned that if the advance to the north was not halted, then 'China will be forced to intervene in Korea'.

It was at this stage that serious disagreements between President Truman and General MacArthur began to emerge. Truman had angered the general when he ordered him not to place American troops on the Yalu river, and things got worse when he refused MacArthur's request to bomb targets in China. General MacArthur did not attempt to hide his contempt for the president.

China's warnings were ignored, and Mao Tse-tung secretly ordered Chinese 'volunteers' to move into the war zone. On 26 November the Chinese forces launched a massive counterattack, so driving General MacArthur's forces back.

Although the war was still technically a civil war between North and South Korea, the reality was now a conflict between China (supported by Soviet weapons and advisers) on the one hand, and the United States on the other. To make things worse, President Truman could not afford to be seen to be giving in to communism; nuclear weapons were available if he decided to use them.

This illustration shows Chinese forces in Korea capturing a US tank.

November – December 1950

By November 1950, the number of Chinese troops in the field was huge (and would eventually reach 1.2 million). The UN troops were swept back by the sheer size of the Chinese force: one US soldier recalled, 'The shooting was terrific, there were Chinese shouting everywhere, I didn't know which way to go. In the end, I just ran with the crowd. We just ran and ran'. Within two weeks, the UN forces had given up all the land that they had gained in

towards America, there was no real sign of an end to the deadlock, and the casualties were steadily rising.

The pressure of the war now began to take its toll on the American leadership. General MacArthur publicly criticised President Truman's tactics, and his idea of a limited war. MacArthur said that he wanted to be given the resources to drive the communists back as far as possible. Indeed, MacArthur even wanted to take on China itself, backed by the use of atomic weapons. Although many of the American public agreed with MacArthur, his plans carried a real risk of a full war with China, intervention by the USSR, and even a third world war.

Truman was furious with his outspoken general, and General MacArthur was dismissed on 11 April 1951 and was replaced as UN commander by General Ridgway.

Summer 1951

A military solution of the Korean War was still not in sight. Both sides had now constructed extensive trench networks; American bombing raids on the north intensified. The temptation to use atomic weapons as a way of ending the deadlock remained.

In June 1951, provisional peace talks began, suggested by the Soviets. The talks were as difficult to bring to an end as the fighting, however, and dragged on for many months.

North Korea. On Christmas Day in 1950, the Chinese troops crossed the 38th Parallel; the UN troops retreated into South Korea. For America, the war was no longer going according to plan.

January 1951

On 4 January 1951, the US/UN forces were driven out of Seoul. Only after weeks of bitter fighting was MacArthur again able to push the Chinese forces back to the 38th Parallel. Although the tide had turned

1952

The peace talks were threatened when a major dispute flared up over the exchange of prisoners of war. In the summer of 1952, America resumed its extensive bombing of the north, which probably helped to encourage the Chinese to agree the terms for peace. On 17 June, a revised demarcation-line (border) agreement was signed. The move for peace was boosted further when Korea became the key issue in the American presidential election in November.

President Eisenhower succeeds Truman

Truman was weary of the war in Korea, and announced that he would not stand for re-election as president. Instead, the election was won by the Republican candidate, General Dwight D Eisenhower. Realising that the American people were sick of the stalemate in Korea, he promised that, if he was elected, he would 'go there' to bring the war to 'an early and honourable end'.

Eisenhower carried out his promise shortly after he won the election. The issue of the prisoners of war remained a problem, however, but Eisenhower brought an end to the deadlock by hinting that he would resort to using nuclear weapons if an agreement could not be reached.

The way was now paved for an end to the war. The peace talks had dragged on from July 1951 until July 1953, and had been marked by bitterness and tension. A cease-fire agreement was finally signed at the village of Panmunjom on 27 July 1953. It is worth noting that even today a full peace settlement has still not been signed.

The end of the war was greeted with widespread relief in the United States, where the war had become increasingly unpopular. Most Americans had expected that their country's involvement in Korea would be brief, and that there would be limited casualties on the American side. But by July 1953 America had lost 25,000 dead, 10,000 missing and 103,000 wounded. Their allies had suffered too: in the process of freeing their country from communist aggression, a total of 415,000 South Koreans had died.

The signing of the peace agreement by American and North Korean military leaders.

The importance of the Korean War

Apart from the Cuban Missile Crisis, the Korean War was the closest that America came to using its nuclear weapons since 1945. It was the only battlefield since World War II in which the armies of two great powers – the United States and China – had fought against each other. For the UN, it was one of the very few occasions on which it was able to make an effective response to an attack on one of its members.

For America, it turned out to be a terribly frustrating war. One American historian has called Korea the 'century's nastiest little war'. Although the objective of forcing the communists out of the south was achieved, the cost was immense. Apart from the massive casualties, the Americans realised that fighting in rural and jungle conditions against a well-organised and fast-moving communist army was a traumatic experience. The most painful part of it all, from the American point of view, was that the American forces had not been able to defeat their communist enemies and thus bring the war to a totally successful conclusion.

The newly elected President Eisenhower and Vice President Nixon in 1953. A cease-fire was signed in Vietnam a few months after Eisenhower's inauguration.

QUESTIONS

1 Explain the importance of the 38th Parallel in the Korean War.

2 Why did President Truman feel obliged to enter the Korean War?

3 Why did the United States receive such strong support about Korea from the UN Security Council?

4 Why did the Chinese enter the Korean War, and what impact did their intervention have?

5 Explain why General MacArthur and President Truman disagreed about the Korean War.

6 Why was it so difficult to bring the Korean War to an end?

7 How far was the Korean War a success for the UN?

10 The Cuban Missile Crisis

Washington, DC, Sunday, 14 October 1962

The sign on the building in central Washington in America told passers-by that it was a car dealership. Hidden on one of the upper floors, however, was a series of rooms used by the Central Intelligence Agency (CIA). Inside a darkened room, photographic experts were straining their eyes over images taken that morning by a U-2 reconnaissance plane. Flying twelve miles above Cuba, it had picked up a great deal of activity in fields near the village of San Cristobal, one hundred miles west of the capital, Havana.

American photograph taken by a reconnaissance plane and showing the development of missile sites on the island of Cuba.

The Cuban Missile Crisis

Soviet missile bases
US territory
US bases

Within hours, the CIA was certain that a site was being prepared for a number of ten-metre-long, medium-range ballistic missiles. Weapons experts knew that these were of exactly the same type that had been paraded past the Soviet president on military processions through Moscow. The USSR, they believed, was secretly preparing to place nuclear missiles on an island only ninety miles off the coast of Florida; New York City and Washington, DC were within easy range. The Cuban Missile Crisis had begun. The world was about to be brought to the brink of nuclear oblivion.

Cuba

Until 1959, Cuba, a Caribbean island close to Florida, had been under the control of the United States. For decades, the White House had lent support to the country's corrupt dictator, Fulgencio Batista. Havana was a popular destination for American tourists, and the Mafia was making huge profits from the operations which it ran there. This relationship changed, however, when Batista was overthrown by a young and popular leader named Fidel Castro.

Fidel Castro

Castro spoke of 'freedom' and 'national pride' for Cuba. He wanted to return the island's extensive sugar plantations to the Cuban people, rather than leaving them in the hands of American businessmen. When Castro visited the USA as leader of Cuba in April 1959, he was given a cold reception: the Americans were alarmed by Castro's ideas. He was given a much warmer reception when he visited the Soviet leader, President Khrushchev (Stalin had died in 1953).

Khrushchev pounds the table with his fist as he addresses the fifteenth session of the UN General Assembly, 1971.

Castro in Moscow in 1963, being greeted by President Khrushchev.

Nikita Khrushchev

The Soviet president had first met John Kennedy at a reception, when the American was still just a senator, and he told Kennedy that he looked too young to be one. After the reception, he sent Kennedy an autographed place card, which read: 'Dear Jack … Maybe this will enable you to get out of jail when the revolution comes'.

Khrushchev was not always so amiable. He liked to project the image of a tough, brash, outspoken and uncompromising leader. In addition, he was surrounded by a number of hard-line communists and generals, who felt that the best way in which to deal with America was to take a tough approach. Khrushchev spoke of Cuba as a 'beacon of revolutionary struggle', and realised the importance of developing a good relationship with Castro. The USSR provided Cuba with aid, military supplies, technicians and arms.

John F Kennedy

Kennedy addresses a news conference.

The Bay of Pigs

- Castro quickly mobilised his forces and pinned down the invaders on the beach;
- the Americans had completely underestimated the level of support which Castro had built up for himself in Cuba;
- Castro used the invasion to whip up patriotic feeling against the invaders;
- the exiles were met with massive resistance;
- more than a hundred exiles were killed, and the rest were taken prisoner;
- the Bay of Pigs was a triumph for Castro, and a humiliation for Kennedy;
- Castro's popularity with the Cuban people now soared to new heights.

Before winning the presidential election of 1960, Kennedy had portrayed himself as a tough leader: 'I have strong ideas about the United States playing a great role in a historic moment when the cause of freedom is endangered all over the world. When the United States stands as the only sentry at the gate. When we can see the camp fires of the enemy burning on distant hills'.

Once elected, President Kennedy wanted to be seen as a man of action. He soon approved details of a plan which had been drawn up by the CIA for Kennedy's predecessor, President Eisenhower. This involved training and arming anti-Castro Cuban exiles at secret camps in Central America. In April 1961, a force of approximately 1500 men landed in Cuba, on the sandy beach known as the Bay of Pigs. The invasion soon turned into a disaster for Kennedy.

The aftermath of the Bay of Pigs

Although the invasion had been a disaster, Kennedy was now more determined than ever to get rid of Castro. Meanwhile, in June 1961, he met Khrushchev at the superpower summit held in Vienna. The meeting was not a success. Khrushchev had decided that Kennedy lacked the experience and strength needed to be an effective statesman. President Kennedy's parting words were that they could both expect 'a cold winter'.

When he returned to Washington, Kennedy authorised Operation Mongoose, a programme intended to remove Castro, funded with $50 million of government money. At the same time, Khrushchev, boosted by what he saw as a personal victory over Kennedy at Vienna, made the decision to deter an American move against Cuba by installing Soviet nuclear missiles in that country.

It was well known that the USA already had Jupiter nuclear missiles based in Turkey, as well as warheads in Italy and Britain. Khrushchev felt that this established a precedent for the stationing of nuclear missiles abroad. In the summer of 1962, Soviet nuclear missiles were therefore secretly moved to a number of Soviet ports, and were later shipped to Cuba. The Soviet leader then spent the summer at his holiday estate on the Black Sea. When he returned, he was tanned, healthy and energetic. He was about to face the biggest crisis of his life.

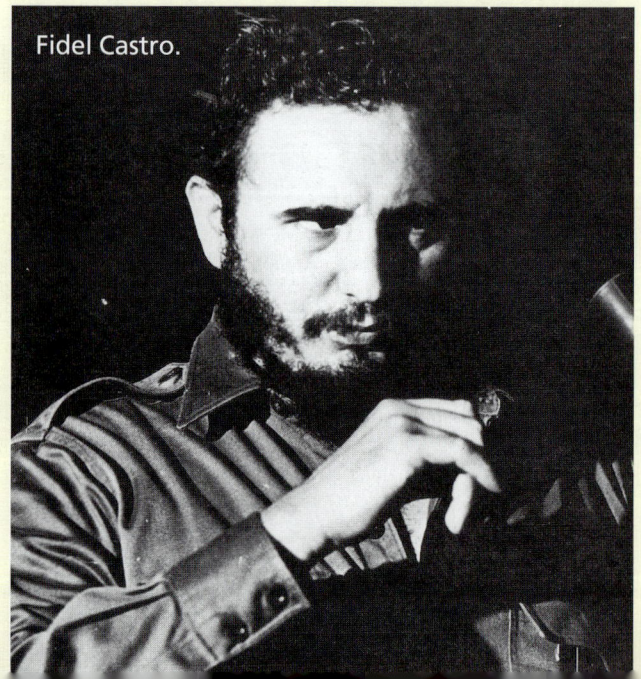

Fidel Castro.

The crisis unfolds

Sunday, 14 October 1962

Following claims by an American politician that the Soviets were installing missiles in Cuba, an American U-2 aircraft took a series of reconnaissance photographs twelve miles above the island.

Monday, 15 October 1962

Defence experts concluded that a site was being prepared for a number of medium-range ballistic missiles. They would soon be operational.

Tuesday, 16 October 1962

Alarmed by the intelligence reports, Kennedy quickly called a meeting of a group of top-level advisers, which included his brother, Robert Kennedy (the attorney general). This group, which met frequently as the crisis unfolded, became known as the Executive Committee (Ex-Comm). One member later recalled that Kennedy was more tense than he had ever seen him, but was also 'absolutely determined that the missiles would leave Cuba'.

Friday, 19 October 1962

Further reconnaissance photos revealed more missile sites, this time threatening a longer range. The experts said that the Soviets were working flat out, and that the missiles were almost ready.

Sunday, 21 October 1962

Kennedy was told by his chiefs of staff that there was no guarantee that all of the Soviet missiles could be destroyed by a single American attack. They said that it was possible that undetected sites might exist, so enabling the Soviets to retaliate against an American strike. Kennedy therefore ruled out the option of a first strike by America.

Kennedy with Secretary of Defence Robert McNamara and Secretary of State Dean Rusk.

Monday, 22 October 1962

That evening, Kennedy went on television to make a live broadcast to the American people. It was probably the most important speech in the whole period of the Cold War.

He announced that Cuba would be 'quarantined' until the Soviet Union removed its missiles from the island of Cuba.

> *This government has maintained the closest surveillance of the Soviet military build-up on the island of Cuba ...Unmistakable evidence has established the fact that a series of offensive missile sites is now in preparation ... To halt this offensive build-up, a strict quarantine on all . . . military equipment under shipment to Cuba is being initiated ... I have directed the armed forces to prepare for any eventualities. Any missile launched from Cuba against any nation in this hemisphere would bring a full retaliatory response upon the Soviet Union ... I call upon Chairman Khrushchev to halt and eliminate this ... provocative threat to world peace ... He has an opportunity now to move the world back from the abyss of destruction by ... withdrawing these weapons from Cuba.*

That night, in the war room of the Pentagon (America's military headquarters), a giant wall map glowed with small lights, showing all the US military bases around the world which were now on maximum alert. The same step was also taken by the Soviet Union.

Wednesday, 24 October 1962

The blockade was in place by the morning. Approximately twenty-five Soviet ships were spread across the Atlantic en route to Cuba. Then, at 10.25a.m., President Kennedy received the most important message of his political career: a number of Soviet ships had stopped dead in mid-Atlantic. A member of Ex-Comm observed: 'We're eyeball to eyeball, and I think the other fellow just blinked'.

Friday, 26 October 1962

Kennedy received a message from Khrushchev, hinting that he was ready for some sort of settlement: the USSR might withdraw the missiles, Khrushchev said, if President Kennedy pledged not to invade Cuba. Before Ex-Comm had decided how to reply, however, a second, more aggressive message was received: the Soviet Union would only remove the missiles from Cuba if the United States removed its Jupiter missiles from Turkey.

The view of the Executive Committee was that the United States could not be seen to give in to Soviet demands 'at the point of a gun'. The aggressive tone of the second message led Ex-Comm to believe that Khrushchev was coming under fierce pressure from hard-line generals to stand up to the United States. The crisis seemed to be getting out of hand.

A US naval vessel keeps a watchful eye on a Soviet freighter believed to be carrying military equipment.

Saturday, 27 October 1962

Castro's troops in Cuba did not know about the messages being sent by Khrushchev. At the worst possible moment, during the negotiations, they shot down an American U-2 spy plane, killing the pilot. Kennedy was stunned. He did not know that the Cubans had acted on their own, without the support of the Soviets. Some of Kennedy's hard-line advisers now urged the president to set a massive military response in motion. The world was now on the brink of nuclear war.

The fears of ordinary people that there would now be a terrible war are described in this extract from a letter written by an American schoolgirl to a friend: 'Can you imagine not seeing another Christmas, Thanksgiving, Easter, birthday, dance or even Halloween? … We're just too young to die'.

Kennedy had already brought his wife and children to Washington, so that they could be moved to the safety of the presidential bunker. Privately, he spoke of his fears that a mistake now would lead to the death of 300 million people within twenty-four hours.

It was at this stage that Robert Kennedy made the contribution which helped to solve the crisis: he suggested that the US should reply to the first message and ignore the second, more aggressive, one. Kennedy's reply to Khrushchev therefore said that the US would promise not to invade Cuba, but could not make a decision about Turkey without consulting its NATO allies. In return for the Cuba guarantee, America demanded the withdrawal of the Soviet missiles from Cuba.

Sunday, 28 October 1962

Radio Moscow announced that the nuclear weapons would be dismantled. Privately, the Americans and Soviets agreed to resolve the Turkey issue, as long as the Soviets did not discuss it publicly. Six months later, the American missiles were removed. World War III had been narrowly avoided.

ASSIGNMENT

1 What are the signs that the world came to the brink of nuclear war in 1962?

2 Explain why Cuba was so important to:
a the USA;
b the Soviet Union.

3 How important was Fidel Castro in the development of the Cuban Missile Crisis?

4 Here are five factors which played a part in preventing the outbreak of nuclear war in 1962:
a President Kennedy's handling of the crisis;
b Khrushchev's fear of the United States' military might;
c Khrushchev's handling of the crisis;
d public opinion around the world was against an escalation of the crisis;
e sheer good luck on both sides.

Write a short paragraph in support of each of these five points. Place the points in what you think are their order of importance, and explain why.

11 American involvement in Vietnam

The background

The war in Vietnam was a tragedy for all concerned: 58,132 Americans were killed, or are still classified as being missing in action; more than 300,000 US troops were wounded; the average age of the American soldiers in Vietnam was only nineteen.

These losses were small in comparison with those of the Vietnamese people: at least 900,000 North Vietnamese combatants were killed, and 2 million wounded (this was out of a total population of only 18-20 million). A further 1 million civilians were killed throughout Vietnam. The South Vietnamese army lost 250,000 dead and 600,000 wounded. Therefore the total loss of life throughout Vietnam reached at least 2.5 million, with several millions more wounded.

Both sides committed terrible atrocities. No image of the war was more horrifying than the sight of a naked Vietnamese girl, with dreadful burns from a napalm (a fiery liquid) attack, running screaming down the road. From the Americans' point of view, it became increasingly difficult to see their young men being killed or mutilated in a country that was thousands of miles away.

Vietnam was once a land of immense natural beauty, but the war devastated the country. Villages were burnt to the ground; napalm was used to clear forests; the chemical, Agent Orange, was used to destroy large areas of jungle; deadly land mines, booby traps and elaborate tunnels remained, even when the war was over.

It is now clear that the war was a devastating experience for both the Vietnamese and the Americans, but why did it happen in the first place?

American troops find an arms cache.

The Vietnam War, 1968

Areas of Vietcong activity

★ Principal US bases by 1968

0   400 km
0   200 miles

These children are fleeing a napalm attack on their village.

SOURCE A

25 Nov 1966

Hello dear folks

It's going to be hard for me to write this, but maybe it will make me feel better. Yesterday . . . my company was hit out in the field while looking for VC [Vietcong]. We got the word that one boy was killed and six wounded. So the doctors, medics and the captain I work for went over to the hospital to see the boys when they came in and see how they were . . .

They told me that they needed someone to identify a boy they just brought in from my company. He was very bad, they said. So I went into the tent. There on the table was the boy. His face was all cut up and blood all over it. His mouth was open, his eyes were both open. He was a mess. I couldn't really identify him.

So I went outside while they went through his stuff. They found his ID card and dog tags. I went in and they told me his name – Rankin. I cried 'No, God, it can't be!'. But sure enough, after looking at his bloody face again I could see it was him. It really hit me hard because he was one of the nicest guys around . . . After I left the place, I sat down and cried. I just couldn't stop it. I don't think I ever cried so much in my life. I can still see his face now, I will never forget it.

Today the heavens cried for him. It started raining at noon today and has now finally stopped after 10 hours of the hardest rain I have ever seen.

Love Richard

Quoted in Bernard Edelman (ed), *Dear America, Letters Home from Vietnam* (1985).

SOURCE B

Dear Ma

Vietnam has my feelings on a seesaw.

This country is so beautiful, when the sun is shining on the mountains, farmers in their rice paddies, with their water buffalo, palm trees, monkeys, birds and even the strange insects. For a fleeting moment I wasn't in a war zone at all, just on vacation, but still missing you and the family.

There are a few kids who hang around, some with no parents. I feel so sorry for them. I do things to make them laugh. and they call me 'dinky dow' (crazy). But it makes me feel good . . .

Love to all.   Your son, George

Quoted in Edelman, as above.

SOURCE C

The average age of the American soldier in Vietnam was nineteen . . . which made him vulnerable to the psychological strains of the struggle.

Stanley Karnow, *Vietnam* (1993).

American casualties in Vietnam; this wounded marine is about to be winched up to a medical evacuation helicopter, while other wounded await their turn.

The origins of America's war in Vietnam

Between 1945 and 1954 France, the colonial ruler of Vietnam, fought desperately to hang onto its prized possession. This effort collapsed in May 1954, however, after a humiliating military defeat: on 7 May, the French army surrendered to the Vietnamese nationalist army at Dien Bien Phu. It was a major triumph for the nationalist army, known as the Vietminh, led by Ho Chi Minh.

The 17th Parallel

The Vietminh and France called an armistice, and agreed a temporary division of Vietnam along the 17th Parallel. They agreed that the Vietminh would control the north, and the French the south, until 1956. Then elections would be held which would unify the country, probably under the leadership of the communist, Ho Chi Minh.

However, the United States and South Vietnam refused to recognise this agreement. They believed that Ho Chi Minh was being backed by his communist neighbours in China. Although President Eisenhower had brought an end to the war in Korea, he now contemplated US involvement in another part of the Far East.

The domino theory

The Americans viewed Ho Chi Minh's success with alarm. President Eisenhower and his advisers were convinced that if Vietnam was allowed to fall into the hands of the communists, then many other countries, such as Cambodia, Thailand, Burma and Indonesia, would follow suit.

This view became generally known as the 'domino theory'.

SOURCE D

To justify his support for South Vietnam, Eisenhower put forward the 'domino theory' – if the first domino is knocked over then the rest topple in turn. Applying this to south-east Asia, he argued that if South Vietnam were allowed to be taken by any group of communists, then the other countries in the region, Laos, Cambodia, Thailand, Burma, Malaysia and Indonesia, would be taken over in turn.

J Simkin, *American Foreign Policy, 1945-80* (1986).

SOURCE E

We shall pay any price, bear any burden, meet any hardship, support any friend, oppose any foe, to assure the survival and success of liberty.

President Kennedy, in his inaugural speech.

SOURCE F

We have kept our guns over the mantle and our shells in the cupboard for a long time now . . . I can't ask our American soldiers out there to continue to fight with one hand behind their backs.

President Johnson, quoted in George C Herring, *America's Longest War, the United States and Vietnam, 1950-75* (1979).

Ngo Dinh Diem

The Americans now placed their support firmly behind the South Vietnamese government, led by an anti-communist named Ngo Dinh Diem. The United States backed him up by providing arms and military advisers to the south. Meanwhile, Ho Chi Minh and the communists of North Vietnam were growing stronger. They prepared themselves for another war with a Western power.

John F Kennedy

There was no reason why President Kennedy should have disagreed with the domino theory: at the time the threat from communism seemed all too real. Read the extract from Kennedy's inaugural speech (Source E) and you will see how important the issue of defence was to the new president.

Kennedy increased US military aid to the South Vietnamese, but at the same time Ho Chi Minh was stepping up the actions of his guerrilla forces (known as the Vietcong, or 'VC') against the South Vietnamese army. To make matters worse, Ngo Dinh

Diem's corruption and brutality was quickly turning his own people against him. Backed by the CIA, the South Vietnamese army therefore carried out a coup and executed Diem in November 1962. By the time that Kennedy himself was assassinated, a year later, he had increased the number of US military advisers in Vietnam from 500 to 10,000.

Lyndon B Johnson

Look at the comment (Source F) made by President Johnson about Vietnam, shortly after he became president of the USA after Kennedy's death in November 1963.

His feelings were strengthened in February 1965, when Vietcong soldiers attacked a US army barracks, in the process killing five soldiers and destroying five American aircraft. Johnson decided that the solution to the problem lay in the massive use of American military technology which, he believed, would force the Vietcong into submission. Johnson claimed that an overwhelming display of American military might would make the enemy 'sober up and unload his pistol'.

The Tet offensive, 1968

The Tet offensive, 1968.

Between 1965 and 1968, the Americans piled on the pressure against the Vietnamese. They launched repeated bombing raids and increased the number of American troops in Vietnam. Many observers thought that it was only a matter of time before the 'poor peasant army of a third-world country' crumbled into defeat.

On 30 January 1968, however, the North Vietnamese launched a massive counterattack, involving more than 80,000 troops. The Tet offensive, launched on the Vietnamese New Year, cost the Vietcong heavy casualties, but they had already inflicted lasting damage to America's morale. Even though Johnson had used massive bombing raids against them, the Vietcong seemed stronger than ever. Many Americans began despondently to feel that the Vietcong were unbeatable.

The collapse of domestic support for the Vietnam War

The Tet offensive made many Americans question the Vietnam War. It was now clear that President Johnson had been unable to defeat the Vietnamese. In 1968, he was succeeded by a man who was determined to get the United States out of Vietnam: President Richard Nixon.

Meanwhile, newspaper reports of the atrocities committed by American troops undermined popular support for the war even more. Every evening, the TV news showed sickening images from Vietnam. In 1970, six American university students were killed during clashes with the National Guard, which had been called in by the president, when they protested against the war.

President Nixon and the end of the Vietnam War

Although Nixon wanted to end the Vietnam War, he was also detemined not to be the first American president in history to lose a war. In his bid to combine 'peace with honour', Nixon unleashed a new wave of bombing against North Vietnam and its capital, Hanoi. Gradually, however, Nixon began to realise that no amount of force would make the communists in Hanoi agree to his terms. The guerrilla tactics of the Vietcong were furthermore demoralising the American troops. By 1970, Nixon therefore began withdrawing his troops, at the same time increasing the bombing raids on North Vietnam: during the Christmas raids of 1972, the bombing reached new levels of intensity. By 1973, both sides were ready to negotiate.

Peace negotiations

After secret and difficult negotiations, a treaty was finally signed in Paris. Kissinger, for the Americans, and Le Duc Tho, for the North Vietnamese agreed that:

- American soldiers would leave Vietnam;
- American prisoners of war would be returned;
- North Vietnamese troops would stay in the south of Vietnam;
- the political future of South Vietnam would be settled at a later date.

Only two years later, however, North Vietnam launched a major new offensive. In the spring of 1975, Saigon, the South Vietnamese capital, fell into the hands of the communists. This meant that the war in Vietnam was finally over.

The Vietnam War was a disaster and a humiliation for America: the richest and most powerful nation on earth had failed in its attempt to defeat the forces of North Vietnam.

Why did America lose the Vietnam War?

SOURCE G

North Vietnam demonstrated great ingenuity and dogged perseverance in coping with the bombing . . . The government claimed to have dug over 30,000 miles of tunnels, and in heavily bombed areas people spent much of their lives underground. An estimated 90,000 North Vietnamese, many of them women and children, worked full time keeping transportation routes open, and piles of gravel were kept along the major roadways, enabling 'Youth Shock Brigades' to fill craters within hours after bombs fell.

American troops fought well, despite the miserable conditions under which the war was waged – dense jungles and deep swamps, fire ants and leeches, booby traps and ambushes, an elusive but deadly enemy.

[North Vietnamese] losses in military equipment, raw materials, and vehicles were more than offset by increased aid from the Soviet Union and China . . . total assistance from Russia and China has been estimated in excess of $2 billion between 1965 and 1968.

George C Herring, *America's Longest War, the United States and Vietnam, 1950–75* (1979).

SOURCE H

General Giap, the Communist commander, discounted 'the life or death of a hundred, a thousand, tens of thousands of human beings, even our compatriots'. During the war against the Americans, he spoke of fighting ten, fifteen, twenty, fifty years, regardless of the cost, until 'final victory'.

SOURCE I

The US army in Vietnam was a shambles as the war drew to a close in the early 1970s. With President Nixon then repatriating the Americans, nobody wanted to be the last to perish for a cause that had clearly lost its meaning.

Stanley Karnow, *Vietnam* (1983).

ASSIGNMENT

Commission of enquiry into the Vietnam War

You are part of a group which has to provide answers to two questions:

1 Why did America become involved in Vietnam?

2 Why was America unable to win the Vietnam War?

Use the material on pages 98 to page 103, and any other useful material you can find, to produce detailed answers to these two questions. You should also choose photographs to go with your written material.

12 The Soviet Union and Eastern Europe, 1948–90

The Soviet Union and its satellite states

In 1945 Churchill had warned the West of an 'iron curtain' which was descending across Eastern Europe. By 1948, the Soviet Union had total control of six satellite states in Eastern Europe. In the period up to Stalin's death in March 1953, there was no sign that any of these countries would be able to escape from the reality of Soviet domination.

Why did these states allow themselves to be controlled so completely by the Soviet Union while Stalin was in power? Listed below are ten factors which played a part in this domination.

1 Stalin's ruthless personality made everyone afraid of standing up to him.

2 The satellite states felt stonger and safer under the control of the Soviet Union than if they had been smaller, independent states.

3 The Soviet army was large, powerful and capable of quickly crushing any uprising.

4 The satellite states had stong economic links with the Soviet Union because they belonged to the communist Comecon (Council for Mutual Economic Aid).

5 The USSR provided aid to the satellite states through schemes such as the Molotov Plan of 1949.

6 All political parties apart from the communists were forbidden in each of the states. All freedom of speech was banned.

7 Those who did try to oppose Stalin were either killed or sent to labour camps.

8 In each country, a ruthless secret-police force followed the orders of the Communist Party.

9 There was a general belief in each of the states that communism was better than capitalism.

10 The people of each state were bombarded with Stalinist propaganda every day. The newspapers and radio were controlled by the communists.

Soviet tanks parade on Red Square in Moscow on May Day 1958.

An image to evoke Stalinist control of Eastern Europe.

ASSIGNMENT

Work in groups of four or five.

1 Read all ten factors in the Datapoint on page 104.

2 Without telling the rest of the group your choice, choose one factor which you think was of vital importance. Take turns to tell the rest of the group which factor you have chosen and why.

3 Repeat the exercise choosing a second factor.

4 Compare your findings again.

5 Now try to list all of the factors in their order of importance.

How secure was the USSR's control of Eastern Europe, 1948–89?

Stalin's body lying in state in Moscow before his funeral.

The death of Stalin, 1953

Many historians have said that it was Stalin's terrifying personality that held the Soviet Union and its satellite states together. Since 1928, he had controlled the Soviet empire with a vice-like grip. In 1953, however, Stalin died from a brain haemorrhage. If historians were right about Stalin, then the Soviet empire should now have fallen apart. At first, things did seem to become more relaxed:

- instead of one brutal dictator, there was now a collective leadership, with Malenkov as prime minister and Khrushchev as party secretary;
- Beria, who had served as Stalin's chief of secret police, was deposed and executed;
- in 1954, the old Stalinist secret police was disbanded and replaced by the KGB, which was run by a committee rather than a powerful individual;

- in 1955, Khrushchev visited Yugoslavia and apologised to President Tito for the way that Stalin had treated his country;
- in February 1956, Khrushchev made his 'secret speech' to the twentieth Communist Party congress, in which he criticised Stalin's policies and his brutal reign of terror. This speech implied that Khrushchev might be ready to loosen Soviet control over the satellite states of Eastern Europe.

This was a stunning speech. For years, not a single word of criticism of Stalin had been heard. As news of the speech spread to the satellite states, demands grew for their greater independence from Moscow. The process of de-Stalinisation was gathering momentum. The question now was whether the new-style Soviet leadership would lose control of its satellite states.

The Warsaw Pact

The Soviet Union introduced the Warsaw Pact in 1955. This was a military alliance joining together the Soviet Union with Poland, Czechoslovakia, Hungary, Bulgaria, Romania, Albania and East Germany. It served as the communist equivalent to the West's NATO alliance. By signing a military alliance, Khrushchev was trying to tie the countries of the Eastern Bloc together. In the wording of the Warsaw Pact, however, he seemed to be treating the satellite states as equal members of a partnership. Some people in the satellite states of the USSR read this as a signal that the time was right to try to break away from Soviet control.

The Hungarian Uprising, 1956

In June 1956, Yugoslavia signed an agreement with the Soviet Union stating that it was possible for satellite states to follow 'different roads to socialism'. In the same month, thousands of Polish industrial workers went on strike, calling for freedom, better wages and, in some cases, an end to the Soviet occupation of their country.

Khrushchev went to Warsaw to settle the dispute. He agreed that the communist ruler, Gomulka, could carry out some reforms, as long as Poland remained loyal to the Soviet Union and the Warsaw Pact. Events in Hungary, however, soon overshadowed the problems which the Soviets had faced in Poland.

The Hungarian Uprising; Budapest in 1956.

Why was there a rebellion in Hungary in 1956?

News of Khruschev's criticism of Stalin and the Polish uprising spread quickly through the satellite states. In Hungary, the people had good reason to listen with interest. The communists that Stalin had appointed to rule Hungary were hated and feared by the ordinary people. Food and other goods had been taken from Hungary to the Soviet Union. The brutal secret police had arrested and imprisoned thousands of innocent people in the name of Stalinism. Under Stalin, the standard of living of the Hungarian people was desperately poor. Now that Stalin was gone, the Hungarian people yearned for freedom, and, sensing a chance that they might be able to win it, seized the opportunity and rebelled against the Soviet Union in October 1956, only to be mercilessly crushed.

The Hungarian Uprising

23 October 1956

Students took to the streets of Budapest demanding a free press, free elections, and the withdrawal of Soviet troops. They found support from the workers on the streets of the capital. A huge statue of Stalin was toppled to the ground and dragged though the streets.

26 October

The despised communist hard-liner, Matyas Rakosi, was replaced as prime minister by the popular figure of Imre Nagy, a communist who sympathised with the uprising. Street fighting flared up between the protesters and the security police. Soviet tanks were sent into the city.

28 October

After talks between Nagy and the Soviets, the Soviet tanks withdrew. Nagy appealed for calm, but by now the revolt had spread. The rebels were encouraged in their actions by sympathetic words from the American president, Eisenhower, who said, 'I feel with the Hungarian people', and his secretary of state, John Foster Dulles, who said, 'you can count on us'.

1 November

Nagy called for free elections and an end to the communist one-party system, and said that Hungary wanted to leave the Warsaw Pact. This was going too far, too quickly, for the Soviets to accept. Khruschev feared that if Hungary was allowed to break loose from Soviet control, then other satellite states would quickly follow its example. Meanwhile, American attention was distracted by a crisis which was now unfolding in the Middle East.

4 November

The Soviet tanks returned to the streets of Budapest in force. The Hungarians battled bravely against overwhelming odds: 'We have almost no weapons. People are running up to the tanks, throwing in hand grenades and closing the windows. The Hungarian people are not afraid of death. We have just heard a rumour that American troops will get here within an hour or two'. The Hungarians made desperate pleas for Western intervention: 'Civilised people of the world! Our ship is sinking. Light is fading. The shadows grow darker over the soil of Hungary. Extend us your aid'. No help came. Eisenhower hated communism, but he feared an atomic war between the superpowers even more. Approximately 30,000 Hungarians perished. Hundreds of thousands fled across the border to Austria. Nagy was arrested and later shot. He was replaced by Janos Kadar, a man whose loyalty to the Soviet Union was not in doubt. A new, Soviet-backed government was installed.

14 November

The fighting was over. An American magazine reported: 'The steel-shod Russian jackboot heeled down on Hungary this week, stamping and grinding out the young democracy'.

Although there had briefly been a thaw between the United States and the Soviet Union following the death of Stalin, the Hungarian invasion marked an end to this. The atmosphere of the Cold War was still as bitter as ever. It now seemed clear that the United States would not risk a nuclear war over Eastern Europe.

Soviet tanks patrol the streets of Budapest in response to the uprising.

S O U R C E   A

23 October, Budapest

Tempers were running high. A few thousand people went to the city park and surrounded the gigantic statue of Stalin. They got a rope round the neck and began to pull it . . . then it toppled slowly forward – laughter and applause greeted the symbolic fall of the former tyrant.

George Mikes, an eye-witness of the Hungarian rising, quoted in Peter Fisher, *The Great Power Conflict* (1985).

S O U R C E   B

26 October

Every street was smashed – paving stones had been torn up, the streets were littered with burnt-out cars. I counted the carcasses of 40 Soviet tanks. Two monster Russian T.34s [tanks] lumbered past, dragging bodies behind them . . . a warning of what happened to freedom fighters.

George Mikes, as left.

1 Work together in pairs for this exercise.

Here are three factors which helped to bring about the Hungarian Uprising:

- poor living conditions in Hungary and a lack of freedom;
- Khrushchev's speech criticising Stalin's methods;
- the USA's encouragement of the Hungarian rebels.

a Firstly, work on your own and place these three factors in what you think is their order of importance.

b Give the reasons for your answer.

c Compare your list with that of your partner and consider the reasons you have each given.

d You now have to agree a joint order of importance.

2 'The Hungarian people were let down by the United States.' Explain why you would:

a agree;

b disagree;

with this statement.

3 'The sole responsibility for the deaths of the Hungarian people lies with the Soviet Union.' To what extent would you agree with this statement? Give the reasons for your answer.

4 'Eisenhower made the right decision not to intervene in Hungary.' How far would you agree with this point of view? Explain your answer.

A statue of Stalin is hacked to pieces in Budapest during the Hungarian Uprising.

Why was the Berlin Wall built in 1961?

Although the West did not intervene against the Soviet Union over Hungary in 1956, the Soviet invasion was a damaging blow to relations between the two superpowers. Even so, Khrushchev told the twentieth Communist Party congress of 1956, 'There are only two ways: either peaceful co-existence, or the most destructive war in history. There is no third way'.

Events in the summer of 1960, however, showed that relations between the superpowers were still poor. On 1 May an American U-2 reconnaissance plane was shot down over the Soviet Union. When, a few days later, the Soviets announced the loss of the plane, the Americans at first claimed that it had been on a weather-research mission. The next day, however, the US was forced to make an embarrassing climb-down, and had to admit that the plane had been on a spying mission. At the start of the Paris summit on 16 May between the superpowers, Khrushchev demanded an apology from the United States. President Eisenhower was not prepared to give this, and the summit talks broke down.

In November 1960, John F Kennedy succeeded Eisenhower as president of the United States. The future of Berlin remained a major issue dividing the superpowers. When Khrushchev met President Kennedy at the Vienna summit in June 1961, he demanded that the Western powers should leave Berlin within six months. Kennedy's parting remark was that they could both anticipate 'a very cold winter'.

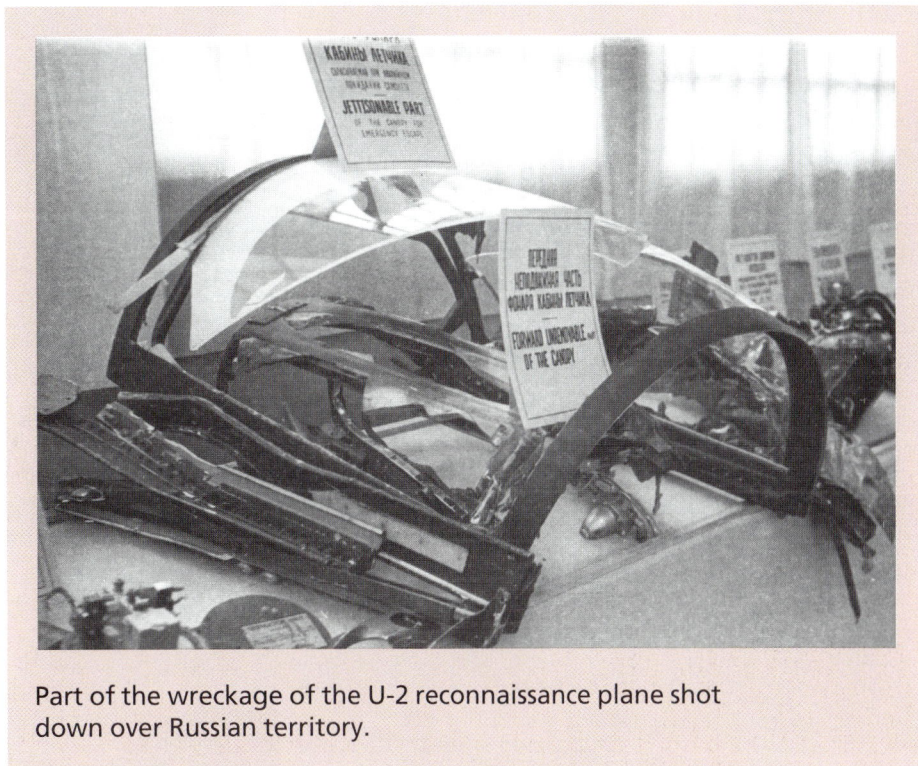

Part of the wreckage of the U-2 reconnaissance plane shot down over Russian territory.

Kennedy and **Khrushchev** at the Vienna summit.

Berlin: city of contrasts

Berlin was becoming an increasing cause for concern and embarrassment to the Soviet Union. Massive Western aid had made West Berlin a wealthy and exciting city. Its shops and department stores were filled with plentiful supplies of food and other consumer goods. In the evening, people were attracted to the city by its bars and nightclubs.

The contrast with the drab streets and food shortages of East Berlin was very obvious. Since 1949, more than 3 million East Germans had escaped through Berlin to the West. Many of East Germany's most able citizens were 'voting with their feet' and leaving communism for the higher living standards and greater freedom of the West. By July 1961, around 10,000 people a week were leaving East Berlin. This gaping hole in the Iron Curtain was causing a serious shortage of essential manpower and threatened the whole economic future of East Germany.

The contrast between life in East and West Berlin.

During the night of 12 August 1961, the Soviets erected a 30-mile barrier across Berlin, cutting off the eastern sector from the West. Huge numbers of police and troops were deployed, backed up by tanks, armoured cars and water cannon. The East German government announced that: 'Measures have been taken … in the interests of peace in Europe and of the security of the GDR [East Germany] and other socialist states'.

Despite Western protests, the East Germans began to replace the barbed-wire fortifications with concrete. A 'no-man's land' of 100 metres was set up between East and West Berlin. Permanently manned machine-gun posts and dazzling searchlights made approaching the wall highly dangerous. All border crossings in the city were closed, and the building of the high, fortified wall made any further escape virtually impossible.

The wall had achieved its purpose: the flood of defectors was reduced to only a small number who were prepared to risk their lives to escape from East Berlin. More than forty Germans were killed by guards in the first year after the wall was built, and many more would lose their lives in later years.

The building of the Berlin Wall.

QUESTIONS

1 What were the main differences between West Berlin and East Berlin?

2 Why were so many people deciding to leave East Berlin?

3 What problems did this create for the communist government of East Germany?

4 Why did East Germany decide to erect the Berlin Wall?

Rebellion in Czechoslovakia

The background

As 1968 began there seemed little doubt that Czechoslovakia's place within the firm grip of the Soviet bloc would remain unchanged. In 1964 the Soviet leader, Nikita Khrushchev, had been replaced by Leonid Brezhnev. Brezhnev was firmly opposed to political change. His priorities were to repress freedom of expression and civil liberties, both at home and within the Soviet empire. Brezhnev believed that the communist parties within the Soviet bloc should show total loyalty to Moscow. While Czechoslovakia was led by the old-style Stalinist, Novotny, this was not a problem. By 1968, however, Novotny was becoming increasingly unpopular with the people of Czechoslovakia. Under his harsh leadership the Czech people had few rights and a poor standard of living. Demonstrations, led at first by students, spread to the streets of the big cities. Novotny stood down and was subsequently replaced by a very different type of communist leader, Alexander Dubček.

Dubček knew that the people wanted to see political reform and a better standard of living. He believed that he could deliver these changes to the Czech people while remaining within the ideals of communism. He called the political freedom which he introduced 'socialism with a human face'. During the early days of the 'Prague Spring', it appeared that the people of Czechoslovakia were finally to be liberated from the harsh control of the Soviet bloc. Hundreds of miles away, in the Kremlin in Moscow, however, the Soviet leader, Brezhnev, watched these events with increasing concern. By August 1968 he was ready to act.

◄ **DATAPOINT** ►

The Czechoslovakian rebellion, 1968

Front page of *The Daily Telegraph*, Thursday, August 22, 1968, with headline "Dubcek arrested by Soviet troops" and "PRAGUE TELLS RUSSIANS 'GO HOME'".

Czechoslovakia and her neighbours

N

POLAND

RUSSIA

EAST
GERMANY

WEST
GERMANY

CZECHOSLOVAKIA

SWITZERLAND

AUSTRIA

HUNGARY

ROMANIA

YUGOSLAVIA

ITALY

BULGARIA

ALBANIA

GREECE

| 0 | 400 | 800 km |
| 0 | 200 | 400 miles |

On 21 August: two burnt-out buses on the streets of Prague, used as barricades in a vain attempt to halt the advancing Soviets, with a Soviet tank positioned behind them.

ASSIGNMENT

1 Using the map and newspaper material on these pages, provide a summary of what happened on 20 August 1968. Include details such as the numbers of troops involved, where they came from, whether they met with any resistance, how far they advanced and if there were any casualties.

2 The first question should have enabled you to deal with the basic information of what has happened. Now we have to deal with the more difficult issue of why these events took place. For this exercise, imagine that your group has to prepare a radio news bulletin on the invasion of Czechoslovakia. Prepare your programme as follows:

a an initial report saying in a dramatic way what has happened;

b an account by your reporter on the streets of Prague, who has to bring the scene to life for your listeners;

c a brief interview with a Czech citizen (anonymous!), who says how they feel about the Soviets;

d an interview with a Soviet politican, who says why the invasion was necessary;

e an interview with an expert on international affairs, who explains why the invasion has taken place.

In order to help you complete this exercise, use the source material and profiles of the two key figures, Alexander Dubček and Leonid Brezhnev, which follow.

Alexander Dubček, the Czech prime minister

Aims:

- he wants to improve living conditions for the Czech people;

- he wants to introduce freedom of speech in newspapers, the radio and television;

- he wants to keep the communist system, but wants it to have less control over people's lives;

- he calls these ideas 'socialism with a human face';

- greater personal freedom is introduced in a period known as the 'Prague Spring'.

Leonid Brezhnev, the Soviet leader

Aims:

- he is determined to keep full control of the satellite states around the Soviet Union;

- he is a hard-line communist opposed to change;

- he is completely against freedom of speech;

- he is surrounded by tough army generals who believe that the best way in which to deal with opposition is to use force.

SOURCE A

We want to set new forces of socialist life in motion in this country, allowing a fuller application of the advantages of socialism.

Alexander Dubček, spring 1968, quoted in Fisher, *The Great Power Conflict after 1945* (1985).

SOURCE B

The word democracy is being misused. There are campaigns against honest party workers. The aim is to end the leading role of the party, to undermine socialism and to turn Czechoslovakia against other socialist countries. Thus . . . the security of our countries is threatened.

Statement issued by Warsaw Pact leaders shortly before the invasion, quoted in Fisher, as above.

SOURCE C

Twice in this century the Russians have had to face an onslaught from the centre of Europe. Only they know the extent of their losses in the last war . . . and the country is still governed by the men who fought it. The Russians have no intention of dismantling their defences in the west.

A historian explaining why the invasion has taken place, quoted in Fisher, as above.

SOURCE D

Tass is authorised to state that the leaders of the Czechoslovak Socialist Republic have asked the Soviet Union and allied states to render the Czechoslovak people urgent assistance. This request was brought about by the threat which has arisen to the socialist system existing in Czechoslovakia.

Statement issued by Tass (the Soviet news agency), 21 August 1968.

SOURCE E

When forces that are hostile to socialism try to turn the development of some socialist country towards capitalism . . . it becomes not only a problem of the country concerned, but a common problem and concern of all socialist countries.

Leonid Brezhnev, quoted in Fisher, as above.

Invasion!

After the people of Czechoslovakia rebelled against the Soviet Union, 400,000 troops were sent into Czechoslovakia on 20 August 1968. The Czech prime minister, Dubček, tried to keep calm: he remembered the bloodshed in Hungary in 1956. The Czech radio urged people not to provoke the Soviets, but to use 'passive resistance' instead; they were told to ignore the Soviets. The Soviet troops had been told that the Czech people would welcome their 'assistance', but some Czechs offered even greater oppostion than just passive resistance. Tanks were set on fire; some people dared to stand in front of the Soviet tanks waving the Czech flag; one student set fire to himself in the centre of Prague as a protest.

Dubček was taken to Moscow to explain himself to the Soviet leaders. When he returned, he was forced to tell the Czech people that the new freedoms would have to be stopped. In the spring of 1969, he resigned his post and was given a job by the Soviets as an office clerk. The Prague Spring had been destroyed.

The role of the West in the invasion of Czechoslovakia

Western leaders looked on in horror as the Czech uprising was crushed. Seventy-two Czechs were killed. The passive resistance of many at least meant that they did not suffer the massive casualties that had been inflicted on Hungary in 1956. In both cases, however, the West had offered sympathy but not help.

In 1968 relations between the Soviet Union and America were delicately balanced. Since the Cuban Missile Crisis, there had been some improvement in relations. The West was not prepared to damage this by intervening on the part of the Czechs.

Soviet troops march through Prague in 1968.

ASSIGNMENT

How similar were the two rebellions?

You have to produce a detailed comparison of the two uprisings in Hungary and Czechoslovakia. Use a double-page spread in your exercise book or use two pages of file paper.

HUNGARY, 1956	CZECHOSLOVAKIA, 1968
1 Date of uprisings	
2 Key leaders of uprisings	
3 Causes of the uprisings (what factors led the people of the country to try to move away from Sovet control?)	
4 Action taken by the countries to disturb the Soviets	
5 Summary of action taken by the Soviet Union (for example, how many troops were sent in? Were the troops sent in straightaway?)	
6 Casualties	
7 What happened to the leaders of the uprisings?	
8 Attitude of the West towards the uprisings	

14 The end of the Cold War

Protest in Poland

Lech Walesa, the leader of Solidarity in Poland.

The leader of the Soviet Union, Leonid Brezhnev.

The leader of Poland, General Jaruzelski.

If, in 1979, the Polish people had been asked to identify the three men shown in the pictures here, they would have had no trouble with two, but would have found one impossible. They knew that the Soviet leader, Leonid Brezhnev, had denied them any kind of political reform. Even though their country was ravaged by poverty, much of its food and resources had been stripped from Poland and taken east to the USSR.

In their own country they feared their hard-line communist leader, General Jaruzelski. They knew that any kind of political disturbance would be harshly dealt with by his elite riot police, the feared and hated Zomo.

The man whom they would not have recognised in 1979 was Lech Walesa, a humble electrician who worked in the shipyards of Gdansk. But within a year he had risen from obscurity to become the most popular man in Poland. He created Solidarity, the first free trade union in the entire communist system. The red Solidarity logo, designed by a sign painter at the Gdansk shipyard, became famous as a symbol of opposition to communism.

Like many other Polish workers, Lech Walesa was poorly paid. Food prices were high; Poland was deeply in debt; its agriculture was backward. The country needed change, but it was still in the grip of Soviet rule.

Solidarity

The communist government in Warsaw did what it was told by its Soviet masters. Any Poles who criticised the government, or complained about their poor conditions, risked arrest and imprisonment. Although the majority of Poles were Catholics, the communists did not approve of their religion. But by 1976 the Polish secret police was finding it more and more difficult to keep the workers under control. Tired of their low standard of living, the Poles set up a workers' defence committee, and demanded the release of arrested workers. In 1979, Pope John Paul II visited the country of his birth and told the Poles that they should speak out. Meanwhile, food prices were higher than ever.

In 1980, the unrest spilled over into nationwide strikes. These had begun at the Gdansk shipyard and were led by Lech Walesa. Solidarity, the trade-union movement that he had created, soon grew until it had a membership of 9 million. The Polish Communist Party was losing its grip. The country braced itself for an invasion from the USSR. Surely the Soviet leaders at the Kremlin would not tolerate a Polish uprising?

The invasion did not come. It may have been that the main reason for this was because, at the end of 1979, the Soviets had already launched a massive invasion in Afghanistan. It was not realistic for the Soviets to act against the Poles while the Red Army was already occupied elsewhere.

Martial law

Even so, the Solidarity leaders still faced trouble. At first, it seemed that they had triumphed: the Polish government recognised the Solidarity movement, and there were jubilant scenes in the Gdansk shipyard and across Poland. While the workers celebrated, however, their leaders were being closely watched by the secret police. Telephone calls were tapped; bugging devices were installed at Solidarity meetings. Then the Communist Party took brutal action: in 1981, the Polish leader, General Jaruzelski, declared martial law (a military rule of law). Political opponents to the regime were either arrested or driven underground. Solidarity itself became an illegal organisation.

Yet Poland's problems could not just be brushed aside. The workers were now deeply opposed to communism; their leaders had been arrested, but their spirit was not broken and their ideas survived. In this way, the Solidarity movement had dealt a damaging blow to the Soviet Union's control of the Eastern Bloc. The name of Lech Walesa was no longer unknown, and eventually he would return to lead his people. On a wall in Warsaw, shortly after martial law had been declared in the winter of 1981, a Solidarity member painted a defiant message to the government, warning it that: 'The winter is yours – the spring will be ours'.

The cracks in the Soviet Union's control over Eastern Europe were becoming more serious. But it was not until Mikhail Gorbachev, a different type of leader, emerged from the Kremlin in Moscow, that the people of Eastern Europe were allowed to escape from the grip of the Soviets in which they had been held since 1945.

Mikhail Gorbachev, the Soviet leader

1931–49

He was born in 1931 in the village of Privolnoye in Stavropol province; his family was poor farmers. His father, Sergei, fought in World War II and later became a Communist Party official. Mikhail started work on the family farm when he was thirteen. His family developed close connections with the Communist Party.

1950–56

He studied law at Moscow University and met his future wife, Raisa. He returned to Stavropol after he had graduated.

1957–78

He worked as a Communist Party official in Stavropol. He showed great promise and was eventually promoted to become a member of the central committee of the Communist Party with responsibility for agriculture.

1980–84

At the age of only 49 he became a member of the Politburo, the most powerful ruling body of the Communist Party. He served under President Brezhnev and President Andropov. Then, when Chernenko became leader, Gorbachev was appointed as his deputy. When Gorbachev visited London in December 1984, he made a tremendous impression. He seemed to be more open to ideas and much more dynamic than the old-style Soviet leaders.

1985

When Chernenko fell seriously ill, Gorbachev displayed his tremendous ability by the brilliant way in which he chaired the Politburo meetings. On the day after Chernenko's death, the Politburo made him its new leader at the age of 54. He now introduced dramatic changes which affected not just the Soviet Union, but the entire world.

1985–89

Gorbachev became the first Soviet leader since 1917 to go out and speak to ordinary people. They told him of their economic despair and he realised that the country was on the brink of collapse. Gorbachev introduced his policy of *perestroika* (restructuring) and *glasnost* (openness). Despite his open methods, however, Gorbachev soon attracted mounting criticism from his own people. They blamed him for the Soviet Union's continuing food shortages and economic problems. Even so, Gorbachev still had enough energy and ideas to make a massive impact on the world. The Cold War was about to come to an end.

Gorbachev and the end of the Cold War

In December 1988 the Soviet leader, Mikhail Gorbachev, made a historic speech to the United Nations. He announced plans to cut his country's armed forces by 500,000 men, or 10 per cent. In addition to these massive reductions in the number of Soviet troops, he told the UN: 'We have come here to show our respect for the United Nations . . . [with] its ability to act as a unique international centre in the service of peace and security . . . It is obvious that the use or threat of force can no longer and must no longer be an instrument of foreign policy. This applies above all, to nuclear arms . . . All of us must totally rule out any use of force'.

The West's positive view of Gorbachev as 'a leader that they could do business with' became even more favourable when Soviet troops were withdrawn from Afghanistan, where they had been stationed since the invasion of 1979. In this way Gorbachev was demonstrating that he was ready to work with the West rather than against it.

Gorbachev and the Eastern Bloc

Although Gorbachev had made a very good impression in the West, he was less popular at home. Ironically, in giving his own people freedom of speech, he found himself the target of an increasing amount of personal criticism. Gorbachev was now blamed by many Soviet citizens for the country's rising crime rate, increasing food shortages and rapid inflation. Ironically, many older Soviet citizens now looked back fondly to the Stalinist period as a time of law and order and stability. They associated Gorbachev with mounting chaos. By 1989 he was facing a major crisis and threatened to step down as leader of the Soviet Union.

Meanwhile, in the satellite states, the frustration of the last forty years was now ready to come to the surface. The economic problems which had developed under communism were more severe than ever. The people of Eastern Europe were desperate for political and economic reform.

This time, however, there was a major difference. Gorbachev showed no desire to use force or intimidation against the people of the satellite states. He was aware that the populations of these states were desperate for reform. Gorbachev did not seem to have the time or the desire to crush any future uprising. He was also aware that the Soviet Union's lengthy involvement in the war in Afghanistan had failed, and that it had been had been costly in terms of casualties and expense.

A S S I G N M E N T

Work in pairs for this exercise.

1 Consider each of the following countries:
   - Poland;
   - East Germany;
   - Czechoslovakia;
   - Hungary.

   It is 1989, and there is increasing discontent amongst each of the Soviet Union's satellite states. For each country shown above, write a brief speech which could have been made at a political meeting, explaining why the country was now ready for reform and independence from the Soviet Union. In each case remember to look at:

   a the attitude of the people of that country towards the Soviet Union;

   b how the country had been treated by the Soviet Union;

   c what had happened in the past when the country had tried to break away from Soviet domination;

   d the economic situation which had developed in the country under communism;

   e how the people would feel about political change and greater freedom of speech.

2 In the case of each country, compare the attitude being shown towards the satellite states by Gorbachev in 1989 with those of the Soviet leadership at the time of any earlier uprisings.

The collapse of the Eastern Bloc, 1989

East Germany

By the autumn of 1989, the people of East Germany were once more 'voting with their feet' against their hard-line communist government. Thousands of people began to flee the country, travelling through Czechoslovakia and Hungary. Massive demonstrations of 'people power' in cities like Dresden, Leipzig and East Berlin led to the collapse of the unpopular and corrupt regime of Erich Honecker. He was replaced by another communist leader, Egon Krenz, who was also unable to turn back the tide of events. In November 1989 the government announced that people could travel freely from East to West Berlin. Finally, and most importantly, bulldozers moved in and the Berlin Wall was destroyed.

Czechoslovakia

The protests of East Germany and Poland soon spread through the rest of Eastern Europe. In Czechoslovakia, hundreds of thousands of people took to the streets, especially in the capital city of Prague. Their protests grew even more intense after the police used violence against protesters on 17 November 1989. Two banned political leaders, Alexander Dubček, the deposed communist leader, and the playwright, Vaclav Havel, appeared in public and urged the crowds to continue their protest. The communist government, led by Milos Jakes, had few supporters; when Jakes resigned, he was replaced as president by Vaclav Havel. Free elections were promised for Czechoslovakia in 1990.

President Vaclav Havel.

Hungary

In the case of East Germany, Poland and Czechoslovakia, the pressure for political reform had come from the ordinary people. In the case of Hungary, it was the government itself which accepted the need for change; the most important figure in bringing this about was the radical communist, Imre Pozsgay. The Communist Party promised its people free, multiparty elections for 1990. The moment that told the people of Hungary that things were about to change came when the huge communist star at the top of Budapest's parliament building was torn down. As was the case in all of the other countries, the Soviet Union did not intervene.

Lech Walesa as leader of Poland.

Poland

At the start of 1989, the Solidarity organisation was still banned and, according to the Communist Party, the existence of the trade union 'was at an end'. As the uprisings in Eastern Europe began to take hold, however, it became clear that Gorbachev was not going to intervene. The Communist Party in Poland realised that it was in trouble, and grudgingly announced that it was prepared to hold elections. By the end of August 1989, the people of Poland had elected Lech Walesa as their new prime minister. Walesa became the first non-communist leader that Eastern Europe had seen for forty years.

The USSR

The changes which took place in the Soviet Union after 1985 under the rule of Mikhail Gorbachev were immense, but moved increasingly outside his personal control. Gorbachev's sincere belief that repression could not continue led to a flood of changes. Gorbachev released dissidents (individuals who had criticised the communist system) from prison and refused to intervene when Poland, Romania and Hungary introduced major political reforms which freed the people from communist control. Gorbachev's popularity in the West was boosted still further by his decision to withdraw Soviet troops from Afghanistan. Most amazing of all was Gorbachev's decision to allow the people of East Germany to take part in reunification with West Germany.

Gorbachev's willingness to disarm and reduce the levels of Soviet nuclear missiles finally led to the official end of the Cold War in 1991.

All these changes led to Gorbachev achieving great popularity in the West, where he was awarded the Nobel Prize for Peace. At home, however, the changes he had set in motion were now ready to consume him. Many people in the Soviet Union used their new freedom of expression to criticise Gorbachev himself. They blamed him for the shortages of food and economic difficulties which still afflicted the country. In addition, the subject peoples of the Soviet Union now began to demand similar levels of independence to those granted to the people of Eastern Europe. Although Gorbachev wanted to reform the communist system in the Soviet Union, he did not want to end it, however. He now found himself outflanked by more radical figures, such as Boris Yeltsin. Yeltsin said that the individual republics of the Soviet Union, such as Latvia and Lithuania, should be either allowed to leave the Soviet Union or to remain only as part of a voluntary association.

Boris Yeltsin waves the flag of the Russian Federation after the coup of August 1991.

Yeltsin was prepared to see the end of the special position held by the Communist Party, and a change from a socialist to a market economy, whereas Gorbachev wanted to preserve the Communist Party and reform the economy more gradually. As political pressure mounted, Gorbachev became the target of a coup staged in August 1991 by old-style conservatives whom he had appointed to government two years earlier. With Gorbachev a prisoner in his own *dacha*, or country home, Yeltsin took his life in his hands. He mounted a demonstration against the coup outside the White House, the seat of the Russian *Duma*, or parliament. It seemed highly likely that he would be killed, but his act of courage was infectious, and he was joined by thousands of people who saw Yeltsin as the only alternative to anarchy or a slide back to the worst days of communist repression. In the face of this increasing level of support for Yeltsin, the leaders of the coup proved weak and badly organised; the coup quickly fell apart, but Gorbachev had been severely damaged. It was clear that popular support lay far more with Yeltsin than with Gorbachev.

Yeltsin decided that the only way forward was to disband the Communist Party and formally end the Soviet Union. On 8 December 1991 he announced that the Soviet Union was to be replaced with a new Commonwealth of Independent States (CIS). On Christmas Day, 1991, Gorbachev resigned. Since then Boris Yeltsin has struggled to resolve the political, economic and social problems of the new federation.

Fortunately, with the exception of Armenia and Azerbaijan, the ending of the communist empire did not result in widespread violence or loss of life. It is clear, however, that the economic difficulties which continue to plague the region will ensure continuing political uncertainty.

Elsewhere, change has continued at a breathtaking pace. The unification of Germany, the collapse of the Soviet Union, and the conclusion of the Cold War ended old problems but raised new issues. As the European Community has become more powerful, questions have been raised about its relationship with the United Kingdom. What changes do you think will take place as we move into the next century?

In January 1996, rebels in the Russian breakaway–republic of Chechnya took more than 150 civilian hostages in response to Russian military intervention.

Index